Work Around Australia

David Sheehan

Global Exchange
Newcastle

Work Around Australia

First published in 2001
Second edition 2003. Reprinted 2004, 2006
This third edition 2007

Published by
Global Exchange Pty Ltd (A.C.N. 006 887 556)
PO Box 852
Newcastle NSW 2300
Australia
Tel: (02) 4929 4688
Fax: (02) 4929 4432
Web: www.globalexchange.com.au

Cover design by Salt Creative, Melbourne.
Text design and layout by Anna Kaemmerling, Global Exchange, Newcastle.
Printed in Australia by the McPherson's Printing Group, Maryborough.

Copyright © Global Exchange

All rights reserved. This book is copyright. Apart from any fair dealings for the purpose of private study, criticism, research or review as permitted under the Copyright Act (Australia), no part may be reproduced by any process without written permission. Enquiries should be addressed to the publisher at the above address. Thank you.

National Library of Australia.
Cataloguing in Publication data:

Sheehan, David, 1966-.
Work Around Australia.

3rd ed.
ISBN13: 978 1876438 234.

ISBN10: 1 876438 23 1

1. Travellers - Employment - Australia. 2. Temporary employment - Australia. 3. Casual labour - Australia. 4. Visitors, Foreign - Employment - Australia. I. Title.

331.620994

Disclaimer
The author, contributors and Global Exchange Pty Ltd believe all information supplied in this guide to be correct at the time of printing. However, the parties are not in a position to provide a guarantee to this effect and accept no liability in the event of information proving incorrect. Opportunities, regulations, organisations and addresses change over time. The listing of organisations in this publication does not imply recommendation.

Dedication

For my daughters, Jenna bear and Indi bindi.

Acknowledgements

As is often the case with this type of book, it has been written with the assistance of a great many. In this case it includes the staff of numerous employment agencies, growers associations, tourist information centres and 'work hostels' along with individual farmers and contractors and others not so easily identified. Bryan Havenhand also assisted in the updating of this edition. To them I say thanks.

Author

David Sheehan began in teaching and health sciences before falling in love with travel. In 1990 he co-founded International Exchange Programs (IEP) with a focus on developing international work exchange programs including the popular summer camp USA program.

David has had a taste of working overseas, having worked with youth at risk in the wilderness of the American 'Boundary Waters' and Canada's Quetico National Park leading canoe expeditions as well as enjoying stints in the wilds of Colorado. Today, he enjoys travelling around Australia and overseas to relax, surf and write travel stories.

As a member of the Australian Society of Travel Writers, David looks forward to freelance travel writing and exploring more off-track travel destinations. He currently operates a business focusing on continuing education for the complementary health industry.

Global Exchange

Global Exchange is a publisher specialising in titles along the theme of 'working and learning across borders' with particular reference to opportunities available to Australians and New Zealanders. Check our website at www.globalexchange.com.au. Current titles with this theme include:

Teaching Overseas for Aussies and Kiwis
Working Overseas: a working holiday guide
Australian Expats: stories from abroad
Volunteer Work Overseas for Australians and New Zealanders
International Careers for Australians
Japan: a working holiday guide
Working in London and the UK
Going Overseas on a Budget: An A-Z (also with the Global Travel Diary)
Inspiring Adventures Overseas: special interest travel
The Independent Hostel Guide for Britain and Europe
Netting a Job in Australia and New Zealand

Feedback

Global Exchange is always keen to hear from travellers and other with feedback on your publications. Change is a constant and no more than in travel.

If you have particular comments regarding this book, contact the author via the publisher at Global Exchange, PO Box 852, Newcastle NSW 2300 or at the publisher's website at www.globalexchange.com.au.

Contents

1. Introduction 7
2. Working the harvest trail 11
3. Maps of Australia 31
4. Harvest trail - Queensland 39
5. Harvest trail - New South Wales 68
6. Harvest trail - Victoria 99
7. Harvest trail - Tasmania 112
8. Harvest trail - South Australia 118
9. Harvest trail - Western Australia 128
10. Harvest trail - Northern Territory 144
11. Resort work 149
12. Casino work 177
13. Ski fields work 186
14. Mining work 198
15. Working in the cities 205
16. Volunteer work 214
17. For working holiday makers 221
18. More information 235
19. Appendix 238

welcome
to the best large hostel in the world!*

wake up!

*and best hostel in Oceania!

More than 500,000 hostel users voted and selected the winning hostels from over 10,000 properties featured on Hostelworld.com

wake up! with someone new
sydney's best budget accommodation

a great place to start your stay in sydney, meet up with your friends or make new ones!

| centrally located | independently run | dorms and private rooms available | secure, clean and comfortable | side bar & café | lockers in all rooms | 2 tv areas | laundries on 6 levels | kitchen

509 Pitt Street Sydney Australia

www.wakeup.com.au

24 hour check-in

call up! 9288 7888

free orientations

accommodation bar café internet

Introduction

Work Around Australia has been written for the increasing number of people travelling and working their way around Australia. As you have read this far into the book you're probably already on the road or at least intending to be there soon. You may be a local who is looking for something a bit different or an international visitor on a working holiday visa or a student visa. Either way, this book will point you in the right direction for work, at any time of the year.

If you plan to travel around Australia on a working holiday visa chapter 17 provides advice that is worth following to save you hassles during your trip. This advice may also be of use for those on student visas who are studying in Australia and allowed to spend part of their time working.

Working while you travel will appeal to your spirit of adventure and allows you to find out about local life behind the shiny tourist brochures. Besides, while you're at it you'll be earning money that can keep you travelling. Many of us dream about leaving a 'day-in day-out' existence, where you rise from your bed each day knowing exactly what's in store for you. Once bitten, you may find that the semi-nomadic life of the itinerant worker is for you, at least for a short time.

While a significant part of this book is devoted to agricultural and horticultural work (now known as the harvest trail), it also covers short-term work in resorts, casinos and on the snow fields. From this third edition there is also a chapter on the mining industry given its insatiable appetite for workers. Short-term work in the cities and opportunities for volunteer work also receive a chapter each. A list of city-based employment agencies is included, with the areas of expertise of each agency listed to assist you in finding work. Most of the larger employment agencies will have offices in several cities, allowing you to easily use their services as you move about the country.

Work Around Australia focuses on where work is and when it can be found. You can use the charts to find out where work is available

at any time during the year. While this book also contains a brief summary of each town's attractions and activities, you may wish to pick up a destination travel guide to find out about the different regions and towns you'll be travelling through. Once you arrive, all but the tiniest of towns will have plenty of information about the area. Certainly you'll need to get hold of a decent map, and if you're travelling by train and bus, the necessary timetables. However, many of the harvest trail destinations require a car for convenience if nothing else—it can be a long way between towns and farms.

Good luck as you work and travel your way across Australia!

Postscript

As this book goes to press, the drought, that has inflicted many parts of Australia for several years, is threatening the supply of irrigation water to some of the crops mentioned in this book. Without significant rains in the latter half of 2007 (which have been predicted by some) many of the crops may not producing as usual in 2008. This will vary from area to area so a more thorough check may be necessary of the areas to which you are planning to travel and work.

Plan your Australian trip online

BUG *(www.bugaustralia.com)* is a brilliant site to help you plan your trip around Australia. This leading online backpackers' resource features:

- extensive destination guides
- information on budget travel options including budget flights around Australia plus Australian bus and rail passes
- forums where you can share advice and travel tips with other travellers
- the original hostel review website with thousands of reviews
- book budget accommodation online with secure online reservations for thousands of hostels and no booking fee for most hostel bookings

BUG's accommodation reviews are focused solely on hostels. You won't find any hotels, motels or fancy resorts – just the web's most comprehensive hostel reviews.

BUG's online hostel reviews are independent. In addition to reviews and ratings by BUG's own editors, it has thousands of reviews written by real travellers and, unlike other hostel sites, BUG never lets hostels write their own hostel description.

Detailed reviews for thousands of hostels worldwide

Explore the world

With guides for destinations throughout the world, BUG is more than just an online Australian travel guide. Visit bug.co.uk for hostel reviews and budget travel information around the world.

bug.co.uk

bugaustralia.com

Working the harvest trail

Work on the harvest trail in Australia is abundant and the availability of jobs will only improve as farmers develop export markets with new and existing crops, expand acreages planted and plant more crops that are labour intensive. To keep up with these developments, farmers need to recruit more labour, both locals and those from overseas eligible to work. Even with the current drought there are many areas unable to find enough labour to manage and harvest crops. One reason is that the resources boom has taken labour away from farming.

A crash course on harvest work

Let there be no misunderstanding, harvest work at best can be described as physically demanding. Apart from the physical work, pickers have to contend with other factors such as the blazing sun, spiders, wasps and other nasty insects, which is why it's of paramount importance to dress correctly for the job.

If you are new to picking then your earnings won't be anything to write home about. Most picking is paid by volume and it takes some practise to get up to speed. Make sure you understand the way you are going to be paid before picking up your bucket. Becoming a quick picker on one crop doesn't guarantee you'll be quick on all crops.

Tree versus ground picking

Tree picking can involve the use of ladders and for some people, the thought of climbing and balancing on ladders all day can be both tiresome and dangerous if you are not steady on your feet. On the other hand, if you suffer from an old back injury, then ground picking can also cause you grief. So be aware of your limitations and carefully choose the type of picking that best suits you. If picking in the field is too much see if you can get work in the packing sheds.

Below is a simple table breaking up crops depending of whether they are 'tree' or 'ground' crops.

Tree crops	Ground crops
avocados, apricots, apples, bananas, cherries, lemons, mandarines, mangoes, nectarines, organges, peaches, plumbs	asparagus, beans, berries, broccoli, cabbage, capsicums, cauliflower, cucumber, corn, cotton, chillies, eggplant, grapes, melons, lettuce, oats, onions, potatoes, pumpkin, strawberries, sugarcane, wheat, zucchinis

Select versus strip picking

Depending on how the farmer will sell the produce, you will be asked to pick either by selection or strip picking. Select picking involves you making a decision on which fruit or vegetable should be picked, according to size, colour, or both! It may take place over a number of weeks as the crop ripens. The farmer will show you samples of what should be picked. Strip picking, as the name suggests, involves taking pretty much all the fruit from a given plant. This is easier than selective picking and the crop is often used for juicing or freezing. Strip picking usually occurs at the end of a harvest and because the picking process is faster, you often make more money if you are paid on the volume you pick.

The Australian climate is known for its harshness. If you are not prepared with the right equipment, you will be exposing yourself to an increased risk from the sun and little critters that crawl and fly around you. In fact, many farmers will not let you start your job without the right gear. Generally speaking, the equipment you require will be cheaper if bought in a large city, so plan ahead before you leave for the picking areas.

Your picking equipment

There's nothing worse than rolling up to work ill-prepared. You'll often be a long way from anywhere so it won't be easy to get the right gear. Make sure you've thought all this through before arriving at the farm gate.

Boots

A 'worn in' pair of sturdy work boots are essential. There is nothing worse than working a full day with blisters from a brand new pair of boots. Buying the boots is only half the exercise, you should make the time to wear the boots in until they soften and are comfortable. If you are working on a ladder up trees you may prefer to have lighter and more flexible boots but ones that have good grip.

Gaiters

Not essential, but a fantastic accessory to have. Gaiters are made of nylon or woven cotton that fit over the ankle and half way up your lower leg. They will protect you from prickles, and 'itchy grass', as well as the odd snake that may be lurking around!

Shirt and pants

If you intend spending long hours picking, think about working in a thin cotton long sleeve top but not so thin that you get sunburned. Shorts don't prevent scratches and insect bites and stings so it's best to wear long pants that are lightweight and of a light colour. Working in the hot sun all day can cause jeans to feel very heavy and hot.

Hat

A good hat that covers both the front of your face, as well as the back of your neck should be one of your closest friends while picking. Sunstroke can occur quickly if your head and face are exposed to the strong sun. Many farmers will not allow you to start work without one, so invest in a hat that is both comfortable and practical.

Rain jacket

Whether you are thinking of working up north in the hotter parts of Australia or down south, a rain jacket will keep you dry while working. Go for a thin material, as bulky jackets will get in your way while working. A rain jacket is to keep you dry while layers of clothes underneath will keep you warm in the colder months.

Water bottle

Drinking water while working outside under the hot sun is essential to your health. Ensure you carry water in the picking area at all times. If possible, attach it to your belt so you don't leave it behind as you move up and down the rows. You should also ensure that it is insulated to keep the water cool. Apart from a small attachable water bottle, it will also become apparent that an additional larger bottle will be needed for longer periods of work. You could get hold of a three or four litre insulated bottle that can be put at close quarters so you can refill your smaller mobile supply.

Sunscreen

If you have travelled from the Northern Hemisphere to Australia for the first time, you'll be in for a shock: Australia's sun causes sunburn quickly, even in winter if you are not used to it. Sunscreen is a must for working outside, even in winter when further north, so invest in a large bottle of the stuff before starting work. Make sure it has a protection factor of at least SPF17.

Insect repellent

If there is a bug that stings or irritates you while you work, you'll find it in Australia! Be prepared and ensure you have an adequate supply of insect repellent such as Bushman or Aerogard with you every day on the job. Also carry something in case you are bitten such as Stingose or After Bite. In some areas the flies can drive you crazy.

First aid kit

You should always carry a first aid kit. A small basic kit is a good investment in case of injury and these can be purchased at the local chemist or outdoor shop. Both St John's Ambulance and the Red Cross sell a good range of first aid kits.

Esky

An Australian word meaning 'portable fridge'. These are usually made of insulated plastic and come in different sizes. You'll need one to store food and drink in to keep cool. Just add ice (though in some places you may need to add ice fairly regularly), but leave it in the shade, preferably where there is a bit of a breeze.

Six hot tips for picking

1. Pick furthest away from the bin first.
2. Never pick from the top step of a ladder.
3. Pick the top of the tree while the bag is light, then work your way down.
4. Pick fruit with the stem attached (no leaves).
5. Pick with both hands – it's faster.
6. Fill empty bags in a gentle way to avoid damage to the fruit. Remember, you only get paid for fruit that will sell.

Accommodation

As outlined in following chapters there are many accommodation options while you are picking and your choice depends on your budget, the time taken to get to work and maybe after hours activities. One of the unfortunate things is that accommodation is often at a premium when everyone's in town for the picking season so the cost of accommodation will often be more expensive than 'out of season'. Before committing yourself to any accommodation check out all charges and conditions.

One type of accommodation which caters for the working travellers is the 'work hostel'. Work hostels often arrange employment in exchange for the worker committing to stay in the hostel. While recognising it only takes a small percentage of operators in any industry to give the rest a bad name there are some 'work hostels' that have practices that could be improved. Some hostel owners set up their arrangements so that it is difficult to break the cycle between work and staying at the hostel, especially in more remote locations.

If you have no prior knowledge of the hostel find out exactly how it works. How many days, if any, do you have to give notice of your departure? Does the hostel provide transport to the farm and if so, is it compulsory to use, even if you have your own transport? How much does this cost? Find out where you can get food and how much this costs? What is security in the hostel like? If you are required to hand in your passport (or in the case of Australians, your drivers licence) is it held in a locked and secured place or is it simply thrown into a draw?

Some accommodation arrangements on farms can also be less than acceptable, not only in terms of the physical facilities, but in terms of the conditions. It may be that you are not permitted to camp but required to stay in accommodation provided by the farmer at a ridiculous price. In some cases such as this, you might end up paying one fifth of your weekly wage into what amounts to rip-off accommodation. You may even be required to pay an additional amount for your hot shower at the end of the day. If you ring ahead to check out work ask some very specific questions about accommodation if you are staying in a work hostel or on the farm. Always get the name of the person you talk to on the phone.

Transport

Although there are comments under each town in the harvest trail section of this book regarding transport, having a vehicle to reach farms is the most convenient, but not necessarily the cheapest way to go. If you have your own vehicle then things are considerably easier than relying on public transport. The national bus company is Greyhound Australia (www.greyhound.com.au) though there are other bus companies that run scheduled routes in regional and local areas. All states except Tasmania have scheduled passenger trains services though these services rarely deliver you close to the action. Websites of each state rail authority are as follows (where websites are split between city and country services, these are the sites with country train information and schedules):

Queensland: www.qr.com.au

NSW: www.countrylink.info

Victoria: www.vline.com.au

South Australia: www.transadelaide.com.au

Western Australia: www.transwa.wa.gov.au

Getting paid

All pickers should have a Tax File Number (TFN) as most employers will ask for this. Australian residents and citizens and those from overseas with a working holiday visa or similar, have different tax rates. Working holiday makers don't receive a tax free threshold for the first $6000 and are taxed 29 cents in the dollar from the first dollar. Working holiday makers should see chapter 17 for more information. You can check the current tax rates on the Australian Tax Office website. Go to www.ato.gov.au then go to 'For individuals' on the left-hand side navigation bar and then to 'Individuals home page', then scroll down to the bottom to 'tax rates'.

The basis on which harvest trail workers are paid varies not only between crops, but can also vary between farms growing the same crop in the same district. Pay can be based on an hourly rate, a weekly rate or a piece rate, which might be a bin, a bucket or a weight. You may find one vineyard, for example, paying an hourly rate while another will pay per bin. If there is plenty of fruit to pick you'll do better on a piece rate than if the fruit is scarce and you need to do more walking and climbing to fill a bin. Some crops need careful picking to prevent bruising and there may be penalties for damage to fruit.

Before beginning work be clear about how you will be paid and when. Where possible find this out before getting to a farm, especially if you are in a position to choose between farms. Picking can be hard work, especially if you are not used to it or to physical work in general. If starting on a new crop then it'll be slow at first with a low pay as well. In fact, some work will never pay well and more than one person has complained of 'slave wages'. Be realistic about your expectations.

Finding out about the harvest trail

That of course, is what this book is about, but there are other sources that are also of use. As a result of a federal government funded project, in mid-2006 the National Harvest Labour Information Service and the Harvest Labour Service were established. Both of these initiatives are intended to make it easier for farmers and seasonal workers to find each other. At peak times farmers often need many more workers than can be found in the local area and word of mouth was proving to be a fairly ineffective way to find the additional labour required. Likewise, seasonal workers wanted reliable information before committing themselves to the expense of travel.

Those looking for work can checkout www.jobsearch.gov.au/harvesttrail for information on work or better still, ring toll free 1800 062 332. In addition to this service there are nominated Harvest Labour Service providers with seven organisations providing services in 16 harvest regions around Australia. These seven organisations are MADEC (www.madec.edu.au), Sarina Russo (www.sarinarusso.com.au), Griffiths Skills (www.summitpersonnel.com.au), Chandler McLeod (www.goharvest.com), Joblink Plus (www.joblinkplus.com.au), CVGT (www.cvgt.com.au), The Job Shop (www.thejobshop.com.au) and Creme of the Crop (www.cotc.com.au). Each of these organizations cover different regional areas of Australia so visit the website to find out the areas and office locations.

Other internet sites providing information on harvest trail jobs

www.austraveljobs.com – most positions are in the north east of Victoria.

www.best.com.au – an employment agency with offices in the New England tablelands and the Gwydir and Namoi regions of NSW and in Southern Queensland around the region of Goondiwindi and St George.

www.bojob.com.au – a website advertising positions around Australia.

www.harvesthotlineaustralia.com.au – a range of rural jobs throughout the country including harvest trail work.

wwww.jobarooo.com – positions around Australia.

www.jobshop.com.au – an employment agency in Perth with jobs in WA and the rest of Australia.

www.pickingjobs.com – an international site with some vacancies for the Australian harvest trail.

www.seasonalwork.com.au – seasonal and short-term work around Australia (with a link to another similar site for New Zealand).

www.waywardbus.com.au – a bus company that takes things slowly but the website has plenty of contacts.

workaboutaustralia.com.au – website with a membership option plus a book by the same name and a jobs board.

www.workstay.com.au – finds positions in WA for a number of occupational groups including fruit picking and other farm work.

Agribusiness organisations employing seasonal labour

There are large agribusinesses employing seasonal labour, the following two are examples.

www.costaexchange.com.au – Costa Exchange is a large and expanding agribusiness growing mushrooms, blueberries, bananas and tomatoes among other fruit and vegetables along with packing, shipping and marketing. Blueberry Farms Australia is now owned by Costa Exchange.

www.mulgowie.com – the Mulgowie Farming Company has 10,000 acres of farmland at Mulgowie near Gatton, at Home Hill and Bowen both in North Queensland and at Boisdale and Lindenow both in the Gippsland area of Victoria.

Individual farms

A few individual farms have websites and the following three are examples.

www.koogiedowns.com – a strawberry farm on the Sunshine Coast in Queensland with picking from July to November.

www.tumbaberry.com.au – a blueberry farm close in Tumbarumba in NSW and one of three blueberry farms now belonging to Costa Exchange, the other two being in Corindi near Coffs Harbour and at Rubus in Tasmania.

www.sgfresh.com – two vineyards near St George in Queensland with grapes for the table and for wine.

Worker hostels

There are worker hostels located in regions requiring seasonal labour. Some of these are listed throughout this book. No doubt there are others that are easier to track down when you are on the road. One such hostel is the Harvest Trail Lodge, 1 Kokoda Terrace, Loxton SA 5333. Tel: (08) 8584 5646. Web: www.harvesttrail.com.

The harvest trail chart

The following harvest trail charts allow you to easily find which picking work suits you best given your travel plans. You can check the months and see where you might find yourself for the best work or you can check the towns to see if there is any picking available when you plan to be there. Either way, work availability might change your plans altogether.

Working the harvest trail

Town	January	February	March	April	May	June
			Queensland			
Atherton	mangoes	avocados	avocados	avocados	avocados	
Ayr					tomatoes, capsicums, pumpkins, melons	tomatoes, capsicums, pumpkins, melons
Bowen					tomatoes, beans, capsicums, corns, rockmelons, zucchinis	tomatoes, beans, capsicums, corns, rockmelons, zucchinis
Bundaberg						
Cairns				hospitality	hospitality	hospitality
Childers	mangoes	mangoes, avocados	avocados	tomatoes	tomatoes	tomatoes
Chinchilla	melons	melons	melons	melons		
Emerald	cotton chipping				vine pruning, citrus fruits	vine pruning, citrus fruits
Gatton	vegetables	vegetables	vegetables	vegetables	vegetables	vegetables
Gayndah	grapes			oranges, mandarines	oranges, mandarines	oranges, mandarines
Giru						
Goondiwindi	cotton chipping					

Town	January	February	March	April	May	June
			Queensland (continued)			
Gympie					beans, squash, cucumbers	beans, squash, cucumbers
Innisfail	bananas	bananas			bananas	bananas
Mundubbera				oranges, mandarines	oranges, mandarines	oranges, mandarines
Nambour						
Stanthorpe	peaches, nectarins, tomatoes, lettuce, grapes	peaches, nectarins, tomatoes, apples, lettuce, grapes	apples, lettuce, grapes	lettuce, grapes		vine pruning
St George	cotton chipping					
Tully	bananas	bananas	bananas	bananas	bananas	bananas
			New South Wales			
Barham	oranges, tomatoes	oranges, tomatoes				
Bathurst	peaches, nectarines	peaches, nectarines	peaches, nectarines			
Batlow	apples, stonefruits	apples, stonefruits	apples, stonefruits	apples, stonefruits	apples, stonefruits	
Bourke	cotton chipping, grapes, citrus fruit	grapes		cotton harvest & ginning	cotton harvest & ginning	
Cessnock	grapes	grapes	grapes	grapes	vine pruning	vine pruning
Coffs Harbour	blueberries	blueberries				
Cowra		grapes	grapes	grapes	vine pruning	vine pruning
Forbes	apples, grapes, pears, tomatoes	apples, grapes, pears, cherries, peaches, tomatoes	apples, grapes, pears, peaches, cherries, beans, zucchinis, peas, tomatoes	cherries, beans, zucchinis, peas, tomatoes		

Town	January	February	March	April	May	June
			New South Wales (continued)			
Griffith	apricots, prunes, peaches, oranges, onions	grapes, onions, oranges	grapes, oranges, onions	oranges	vine pruning	vine pruning
Hillston	oranges, potatos	oranges	oranges	oranges	oranges, potatos	oranges, potatos
Leeton	oranges	grapes, oranges & stone fruits	grapes, oranges & stone fruits	oranges	oranges	
Moree	cotton chipping	cotton chipping		cotton harvest & ginning	cotton harvest & ginning	cotton harvest & ginning
Narromine	cotton chipping	cotton chipping		cotton harvest & ginning	citrus fruits, cotton ginning	citrus fruits
Orange	cherries	apples, pears, grapes	apples, pears, grapes	apples, pears, grapes		
Tumut	cherries, stone fruits	apples, pears, stone fruits	apples, pears, stone fruits	apples, pears, stone fruits	apples, pears	
Wentworth	citrus fruits, vegetables	grapes, vegetables	grapes	grapes	grapes, citrus fruits, vegetables	vine pruning, citrus fruits, vegetables
Young		prunes	prunes			
			Victoria			
Cobram	pears, peaches, apricots	pears, peaches, apricots	pears, peaches, apricots			
Echuca		tomatoes	tomatoes	tomatoes		
Mildura	grapes, citrus fruits	grapes, citrus fruits	grapes, citrus fruits	grapes, citrus fruits		vine pruning
Robinvale	grapes	grapes, vegetables	grapes, vegetables	grapes, vegetables		
Rochester		tomatoes, grapes, olives	tomatoes, grapes, olives	tomatoes, grapes, olives		

Town	January	February	March	April	May	June
			Victoria (continued)			
Shepparton	pears, peaches, apples	pears, peaches, apples, tomatoes	pears, peaches, apples, tomatoes	tomatoes		
Swan Hill	stone fruit	grapes, vegetables, stone fruit	grapes, vegetables, stone fruit	grapes, vegetables, stone fruit		pruning
Wangaratta	stones fruits	grapes, stone fruits	grapes, stone fruits	grapes		vine pruning, stone fruits
Yarra Valley		grapes, apples, pears	grapes, apples, pears	grapes		
			Tasmania			
Gunns Plain	cherries, raspberries, strawberries, capsicums, beans, zucchinis, squash, pumpkins, flowers	capsicums, beans, zucchinis, squash, onions, pumpkins	capsicums, beans, zucchinis, squash, onions, pumpkins	capsicums, beans, zucchinis, squash, onions, pumpkins		
Huon Valley	pears, apples, cherries	pears, apples, cherries	pears, apples, cherries	pears, apples, cherries		
Tamar Valley		grapes, apples	grapes, apples	grapes, apples	grapes, apples	
			South Australia			
Adelaide Hills	strawberries	apples, pears, strawberries	apples, pears	apples, pears		
Barossa Valley	hospitality	grapes	grapes	grapes		vine pruning
Berri and Loxton	oranges, tree pruning, juicing & packing, apricots	oranges, tree pruning, juicing & packing, apricots, dried fruits, peaches, grapes	oranges, tree pruning, juicing & packing, apricots, dried fruits, peaches, grapes	oranges, tree pruning, juicing & packing, apricots, dried fruits, peaches, grapes		oranges, tree pruning

Working the harvest trail

Town	January	February	March	April	May	June
			South Australia (continued)			
Clare		grapes	grapes	grapes		vine pruning
			Western Australia			
Albany	hospitality	grapes	grapes	grapes		
Broome					hospitality	hospitality
Carnarvon			fishing	fishing	fishing	fishing, capsicums, tomatoes, bananas
Donnybrook	apples	apples	apples	apples		
Esperance	sheep, hospitality	sheep, hospitality	sheep	sheep		
Kalgoorlie					hospitality	hospitality
Katanning	sheep	sheep	sheep	sheep		
Kununurra	bananas	bananas	bananas	bananas	zucchinis, squash, watermelons, rockmelons, bananas	zucchinis, squash, watermelons, rockmelons, bananas
Manjimup	vegetables	grapes, vegetables	apples, vegetables, grapes	apples, vegetables, grapes	apples, vegetables	apples, vegetables
Margaret River	hospitality	grapes	grapes	grapes		
Pemberton		apples, grapes	apples, grapes	apples, grapes	apples	apples
			Northern Territory			
Alice Springs					hospitality	hospitality
Darwin					hospitality	hospitality
Katherine						

Queensland

Town	July	August	September	October	November	December
Atherton			tobacco	tobacco	tobacco	mangoes, tobacco
Ayr	tomatoes, capsicums, pumpkins, melons	tomatoes, capsicums, pumpkins, melons	tomatoes, capsicums, pumpkins, melons	sugarcane	mangoes, sugarcane	mangoes, sugarcane
Bowen	tomatoes, beans, capsicums, corns, rockmelons, zucchinis	tomatoes, beans, capsicums, corns, rockmelons, zucchinis	tomatoes, beans, capsicums, corns, rockmelons, zucchinis & tobbaco	tomatoes, beans, capsicums, corns, rockmelons, zucchinis & tobbaco	tomatoes, beans, capsicums, corns, rockmelons, zucchinis & tobbaco	mangoes, tobacco
Bundaberg	tomatoes, capsicums, beans, zucchinis, squash, pumpkins, peas, melons	tomatoes, capsicums, beans, zucchinis, squash, pumpkins, peas, melons	tomatoes, capsicums, beans, zucchinis, squash, pumpkins, peas, melons	tomatoes, capsicums, beans, zucchinis, squash, pumpkins, peas, melons	tomatoes, capsicums, beans, zucchinis, squash, pumpkins, peas, melons	tomatoes, capsicums, beans, zucchinis, squash, pumpkins, peas, melons
Cairns	hospitality, fishing trawlers	hospitality, fishing trawlers	hospitality, fishing trawlers	hospitality		
Childers	tomatoes	tomatoes	tomatoes	zucchini	zucchini	zucchini
Chinchilla					melons	melons
Emerald	citrus fruits, melons	citrus fruits, melons	melons	melons, cotton chipping, grapes	cotton chipping, grapes	citrus fruits
Gatton	vegetables	vegetables	vegetables	vegetables	vegetables	vegetables
Gayndah	oranges, mandarines	oranges, mandarines	oranges, mandarines			grapes
Giru					mangoes	mangoes
Goondiwindi					cotton chipping	cotton chipping

Town	July	August	September	October	November	December
			Queensland (continued)			
Gympie	beans, squash, cucumbers	beans, squash, cucumbers	beans, squash, cucumbers	beans, squash, cucumbers	beans, squash, cucumbers	
Innisfail	bananas	bananas	bananas	bananas	bananas	bananas
Mundubbera	oranges, mandarines	oranges, mandarines	oranges, mandarines	oranges, mandarines		
Nambour		strawberries	strawberries	strawberries	strawberries	
Stanthorpe	vine pruning	vine pruning				
St George					cotton chipping, grapes	cotton chipping, grapes
Tully	bananas	bananas	bananas, melons	bananas, melons	bananas, melons	bananas, melons
			New South Wales			
Barham						oranges, tomatoes
Bathurst				hospitality		peaches, nectarines
Batlow						apples, stonefruits
Bourke	vine pruning	vine pruning	vine pruning		cotton chipping, grapes, citrus fruit	cotton chipping, grapes, citrus fruit
Cessnock	vine pruning	vine pruning				
Coffs Harbour					blueberries	blueberries
Cowra	vine pruning	vine pruning	asparagus	asparagus	asparagus	asparagus
Forbes				asparagus	asparagus, tomatoes, apples, pears	asparagus, tomatoes, apples, pears

Town	July	August	September	October	November	December
New South Wales (continued)						
Griffith	vine pruning	vine pruning			onions	onions
Hillston	oranges, potatoes	potatoes	oranges, potatoes	oranges, potatoes	oranges, potatoes	oranges, potatoes
Leeton	vine pruning	vine pruning				oranges
Moree	cotton ginning		cotton chipping	cotton chipping	cotton chipping	cotton chipping
Narromine	citrus fruits	citrus fruits	citrus fruits, cotton ginning	citrus fruits, cotton ginning	citrus fruits, cotton ginning	citrus fruits, cotton ginning
Orange					cherries	cherries
Tumut					stone fruits	cherries, stone fruits
Wentworth	vine pruning, citrus fruits, vegetables	vine pruning, citrus fruits, vegetables	citrus fruits, vegetables	citrus fruits, vegetables	citrus fruits, vegetables	vine pruning, citrus fruits, vegetables
Young					cherries	cherries
Victoria						
Cobram						pears, peaches, apricots
Echuca				strawberries	strawberries, tomato weeding	strawberries, tomato weeding
Mildura	vine pruning	vine pruning				
Robinvale						
Rochester					tomato weeding	tomato weeding

Town	July	August	September	October	November	December
			Victoria (continued)			
Shepparton						pears, peaches
Swan Hill	pruning	pruning				
Wangaratta	vine pruning, stone fruits	vine pruning, stone fruits			stone fruits	stone fruits
Yarra Valley					cherries	cherries
			Tasmania			
Gunns Plain						raspberries, cherries, strawberries
Huon Valley						flowers, cherries
Tamar Valley	vine pruning	vine pruning	vine pruning			
			South Australia			
Adelaide Hills				strawberries	strawberries	strawberries
Barossa Valley	vine pruning	vine pruning				hospitality
Berri and Loxton	oranges, tree pruning	oranges, tree pruning	oranges, tree pruning, juicing & packing	oranges, tree pruning, juicing & packing	oranges, tree pruning, juicing & packing	oranges, tree pruning, juicing & packing, apricots

Town	July	August	September	October	November	December
			South Australia (continued)			
Clare	vine pruning	vine pruning				
			Western Australia			
Albany					hospitality	hospitality
Broome	hospitality	hospitality	hospitality			
Carnarvon	fishing, capsicums, tomatoes, bananas	fishing, capsicums, tomatoes, bananas	fishing, capsicums, tomatoes, bananas	fishing, capsicums, tomatoes, bananas	fishing, capsicums, tomatoes, bananas	fishing, capsicums, tomatoes, bananas
Donnybrook						
Esperance	sheep	sheep	sheep, hospitality	sheep, hospitality	hospitality, barley, wheat	hospitality, barley, wheat
Kalgoorlie	hospitality	hospitality	hospitality			
Katanning	sheep	sheep	sheep	sheep		
Kununurra	zucchinis, squash, watermelons, rockmelons, bananas	zucchinis, squash, watermelons, rockmelons, bananas	zucchinis, squash, watermelons, rockmelons, mangoes, bananas	zucchinis, squash, watermelons, rockmelons, mangoes, bananas	mangoes, bananas	
Manjimup	vegetables	vegetables	vegetables	vegetables	vegetables	vegetables
Margaret River	pruning vines	pruning vines				hospitality
Pemberton	apples, pruning vines	pruning vines				
			Northern Territory			
Alice Springs	hospitality	hospitality	hospitality	grapes	grapes	grapes
Darwin	hospitality	hospitality	hospitality	mangoes	mangoes	
Katherine			mangoes	mangoes, melons	mangoes, melons	melons

Maps of Australia

Queensland

New South Wales

Victoria

Tasmania

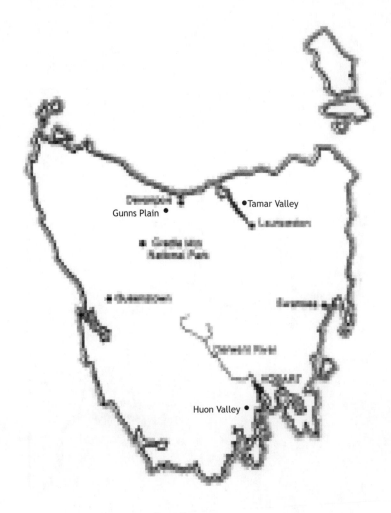

South Australia

Western Australia

Northern Territory

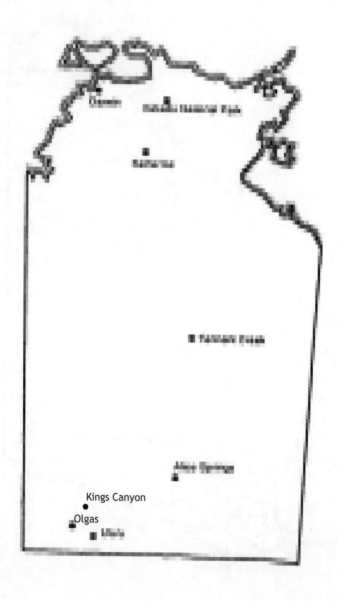

Harvest trail - Queensland

Atherton

The town of Atherton is approximately 80 km south-west of Cairns and represents many opportunities to the working traveller, covering a variety of crops for many months of the year. For this reason, it is very popular with local pickers and overseas backpackers with work visas. Apart from employment opportunities, Atherton and the surrounding areas, which make up the Atherton Tableland, offer a wealth of attractions including rainforests and Aboriginal art and culture along with many interesting small towns.

Type of work

Tobacco, mangoes and avocados are among the largest crops in the area. During September to December you'll find work on tobacco farms, although some prior experience may be necessary to snare a job. Be willing to take a little time to be trained if this is work that you'd like to try.

Avocado season is February to June and quite a number of pickers are required for work in the region. Occasional packing shed work is also available. The mango season takes place between November and April and conditions can be wet and humid, but work is plentiful.

Approximate numbers

The tobacco harvest requires at least 400 workers throughout the season while the avocado season requires approximately 150 workers. The mango harvest requires 200 to 300 workers depending on the quality of the season and, due to the sensitive nature of the fruit, experienced pickers are preferred.

Accommodation

Atherton Backpackers. Tel: (07) 4091 3552.

Atherton Woodlands Caravan Park. Tel: (07) 4091 1407.

Transport

You will need you own transport.

Contacts

Avocado Growers Association, Atherton Tableland, Kairi QLD 4872. Tel: (07) 4095 8121

Tourist Information. Tel: (07) 4051 3588.

Activities while you are there

Try the steam train ride in Herberton, which is operated by volunteers and is the only full-size steam locomotive in North Queensland. Crystal Caves is in the town itself and houses fossils, minerals and giant crystals from around the world. Additionally, if you are visiting the area in September, take part in the Maize Festival or the Tableland Folk Festival in October.

Ayr

Ayr is located 1276 km north of Brisbane and is known for its sugarcane. The town is flanked by the Burdekin River, as well as the beach, so tourists have the best of both fresh and salt water activities including fishing and swimming. The township of Ayr has had a fairly ordinary relationship with the natural elements, having being wiped out in 1903 and severely damaged in 1959 by cyclones.

Type of work

If you have experience driving harvesters, then work on the sugarcane plantations may be on offer. Between May and September you can find picking on vegetable and melon crops around the area. Mangoes are harvested during November and December.

Approximate numbers

300 pickers are required for the melon and vegetable harvest while 300 to 400 pickers are required for mangoes late in the year.

Accommodation

Bartons Caravan Park. Tel: (07) 4782 1101.

Silver Link Caravan Park. Tel: (07) 4783 3933.

Transport
You will need your own transport.

Contacts
Burdekin Mango Growers Association, Ayr QLD 4807.

Tourist Information. Tel: (07) 4771 3061.

Fruit and vegetable growers
Butlers Bananas, 163 Beach Road, Ayr QLD 4807. Tel: (07) 4783 3337.

Paradise Estate Produce, 27 Lisa Avenue, Ayr QLD 4807. Tel: (07) 4783 4585.

Valleyfield Vegetable Growers, Parker Road, Ayr QLD 4807. Tel: (07) 4783 4106.

Activities while you are there
Activities include water sports and a visit to the Ayr Nature Display, where you can see many collections of butterflies, rocks and native fauna.

Bowen

Bowen has a population of 13,400 and is situated 1162 km north of Brisbane. The town's name was derived from Queensland's first governor, George Bowen, and was first settled in 1861. Bowen's claim to fame is its average daily sunshine, which falls just under eight hours a day, which makes it a haven for tourists in winter months and a great environment in which to grow produce.

Due to the vast amount of work available during certain times of the year, Bowen's international backpacker industry is very large, giving the town a truly cosmopolitan mix of cultures during harvest times.

Type of work
Between May and November, Bowen and surrounding areas are a mass of tourists and working travellers, making the most of a huge fruit and vegetable industry. Produce includes tomatoes, cucumbers, beans, capsicums, corn, rockmelons and zucchinis.

In November the mango harvest begins and lasts through until Christmas.

Approximate numbers

Because of the large number of workers required, the figure during the May to November/December period can be more than 5000.

Accommodation

Barnacle Backpackers, 16 Gordon Street, Bowen QLD 4805. Tel: 1800 819 883.

Bowen Backpackers, 56 Herbert Street, Bowen QLD 4805. Tel: (07) 4786 3433.

Queens Beach Caravan Park. Tel: (07) 4785 1313.

Trinity's at the Beach, 93 Horseshoe Bay Road, Bowen QLD 4805. Tel: (07) 4786 4199.

Transport

Daily bus services operate from Brisbane and Cairns.

Contacts

Allison K & L, Collinsville Road, Delta QLD 4805. Tel: (07) 4785 2167.

Castorina S & G, Bruce Highway, Gumlu QLD 4805. Tel: (07) 4784 8141.

Elphinstone & Kirby, 'Leslie', Mt Dangar QLD 4805. Tel: (07) 4785 2244.

Tourist Information. Tel: (07) 4786 4494.

Activities while you are there

Activities include fishing, water sports and visits to the Great Barrier Reef.

Bundaberg

Bundaberg is located 368 km north of Brisbane and offers the working traveller an abundance of work options from July right through until December. Apart from fruit and vegetables, Bundaberg is famous for its rum, while other industries include timber, sugar and beef. It is also the southern entry point to the Great Barrier Reef and therefore is a very popular holiday destination particularly for those from Brisbane.

Type of work

The main work available in and around the Bundaberg region is picking tomatoes and other vegetables. The tomato harvest starts in July and work can be found right through until early December. Other vegetables including capsicums, beans, zucchinis, squash, pumpkins and peas are also harvested during the August to December period. Additionally, Bundaberg also produces melons and workers are needed during this harvest period, starting in November and finishing up around Christmas.

Approximate numbers

The Bundaberg region requires over 2000 workers for the various harvests. The area is very popular with overseas backpackers who are working so try to reach the area at the beginning of the season.

Accommodation

Bundaberg Backpackers & Travellers Lodge, 2 Crofton Street, Bundaberg QLD 4670. Tel: (07) 4152 2080.

City Centre Backpackers, 216 Bourbong Street, Bundaberg QLD 4670. Tel: (07) 4151 3501.

Federal Guesthouse, 221 Bourbong Street, Bundaberg QLD 4670. Tel: (07) 4153 3711.

Nomads Fraser Magic Backpackers, 369 The Esplanade, Bundaberg QLD 4670. Tel: 1800 819 883.

Nomads Bundaberg Workers & Divers Hostel, 64 Barolin Street, Bundaberg QLD 4670. Tel: 1800 819 883.

Prince of Wales Backpackers, 22 Princess Street, Bundaberg QLD 4670. Tel: (07) 4151 1422.

Transport

Bus and train services operate from Cairns and Brisbane.

Contacts

Burnett Valley Olive Growers Association Inc, Kingaroy QLD 4610. Tel: (07) 4162 5856.

Tourist Information. Tel: (07) 4152 2333.

Fruit and vegetable growers

Bundaberg Fruit & Vegetable Growers, 27 Barolin Street, Bundaberg QLD 4670. Tel: (07) 4153 3007.

Moorland Produce, MS 299 Quinns Road, Bundaberg QLD 4670. Tel: (07) 4156 1518.

Read N, Toll's Road, Meadowvale QLD 4670. Tel: (07) 4159 9365.

Schmidt R & B, 'Bonna Fields', Schmidts Road, Bundaberg QLD 4670. Tel: (07) 4155 1792.

CPH Fresh, 49 Hanbury Street, North Bundaberg QLD 4670. Tel: (07) 4151 7777.

Lyne Harvesting, MS 2215 Bonna Road, Bundaberg QLD 4670. Tel: (07) 4155 1253.

Dascombe's Galaxy Farming, 'Bunya View', Minmore Road, Kumbia QLD 4610. Tel: (07) 4164 4210.

Golden Mile Orchards (Qld), 2 Durong Road, Mundubbera QLD 4626. Tel: (07) 4165 4555.

Hidden Valley Dragon Fruit, 524 Turtle Creek Road, Harlin QLD 4306. Tel: (07) 5423 5035.

Peak Crossing Pawpaw Farm, Washpool Road, Peak Crossing QLD 4306.Tel: (07) 5467 2030.

Simpson Farms, Goodwood Plantation, Goodwood Road, Childers QLD 4660. Tel: (07) 4126 8200.

SP Exports, 9 North South Road, Isis Central Mill QLD 4660. Tel: (07) 4126 6333.

Wodonga Park Fruit & Nuts, Crows Nest Road, Blackbutt QLD 4306. Tel: (07) 4163 0166.

Mushroom growers

Bundaberg Mushrooms, Mt Perry Road, Sharon QLD 4670. Tel: (07) 4159 9444.

Chermond Mushroom Farm, Moore Park Road, Bundaberg QLD 4670. Tel: (07) 4159 9713.

Crows Nest Mushrooms, 1 Back Creek Road, Crows Nest QLD 4355. Tel: (07) 4698 1858.

Activities while you are there

The clean, white beaches near neighbouring towns including Innes Park and Burnett Heads are worth the drive. With the Great Barrier Reef nearby, a day cruise out to the coral cays is something not to be missed. Other activities include whale watching (September to October), fishing and other water sports.

Cairns

Cairns has a population of 101,000 and is the gateway to Far North Queensland. As a holiday destination during the winter months, Cairns offers so much in such a small area. For instance, it's just a short drive north to Port Douglas, and a little further on to the famous World Heritage listed Daintree Rainforest. You can catch a day cruise out to the Great Barrier Reef and go snorkelling or scuba diving.

Type of work

For the working traveller, Cairns offers work mainly in the tourism industry, with many bars, restaurants and holiday resorts that cater for a large domestic and international visitor market. Just because you have no experience, or don't wish to work behind a bar or wait on tables, don't assume that there are no other opportunities. On the contrary, resorts for instance need teams of trades people, gardeners, front of house staff, recreation staff and so on. For further information about work opportunities in resorts, refer to chapter 11 for a listing of resorts that regularly require casual and seasonal employees.

Apart from work in the tourism industry, Cairns can offer a unique work experience on the many prawn trawlers which work out of Cairns mainly in the winter months. The work is physical and in many cases your work is rewarded by a warm bed and meals, so this isn't a get rich quick scheme. Rather, it is an opportunity to do something that you would normally not contemplate, so go for it and approach the boats directly, the owners can only say 'no'. However, get a good feel for the owner and crew before making a final decision.

Approximate numbers

The tourism and hospitality industry requires more than 4000 workers every year in a range of positions. This figure includes those positions on the resort islands off Cairns.

Accommodation

Captain Cook Backpackers Resort, 204-212 Sheridan Street, Cairns QLD 4870. Tel: (07) 4051 6811.

Fitzroy Island Resort, Fitzroy Island, Cairns QLD 4870. Tel: (07) 4051 9588.

Hostel 89, 89 The Esplanade, Cairns QLD 4870. Tel: (07) 4031 7477.

Jimmy's on the Esplanade, 83 The Esplanade, Cairns QLD 4870. Tel: (07) 4031 6884.

JJ's Backpackers Hostel, 11-13 Charles Street, Cairns QLD 4870. Tel: (07) 4051 7642.

McLeod Street YHA, 20-24 McLeod Street, Cairns QLD 4870. Tel: (07) 4051 0772.

Nomads Utopia, 702 Bruce Highway, Cairns QLD 4870. Tel: 1800 354 599.

Queens Court, 167-171 Sheridan Street, Cairns QLD 4870. Tel: (07) 4051 7722.

Rosie's Backpackers, 155 The Esplanade, Cairns QLD 4870. Tel: (07) 4051 0235.

Ryan's Rest, 18 Terminus Street, Cairns QLD 4870. Tel: (07) 4051 4734.

The International Hostel, 67-69 The Esplanade, Cairns QLD 4870. Tel: (07) 4031 1545.

YHA on the Esplanade, 93 The Esplanade, Cairns QLD 4870. Tel: (07) 4031 1919.

Transport

Trains, planes and buses operate from Brisbane.

Contacts

Refer to chapter 11 and also visit the prawning boats.

Activities while you are there

Activities include white-water rafting down the nearby Tully River, hot air ballooning, diving, snorkelling, fishing, swimming, visiting galleries and crocodile farms, bushwalking, golf and many others.

Childers

Located on the Bruce Highway some 325 km north of Brisbane, 60 km north of Maryborough and 52 km south of Bundaberg, Childers has traditionally been a centre for sugar cane growing. In recent years there has been considerable development in vegetable production along with promotion of the town as a tourist destination. The town has been declared a National Trust town, a tribute to the historical buildings that line its streets. Even the old Brazilian Leopard trees in the main street are worth pondering.

Type of work

The main vegetable crop is tomatoes and this is where most work is found through there are smaller crops of other vegetables and fruit including avocado, mango and zucchini. The tomatoes are shipped to both domestic and overseas markets.

Approximate numbers

Several hundred pickers and packers are required during the months of April through to September for the tomato crop.

Accommodation

There is a wide choice of hotels, motels, hostels and camping grounds to choose from.

Transport

Buses pass through to and from Brisbane daily and trains stop at nearby towns including Bundaberg and Howard.

Contacts

Grunt Labour Services, 86 Churchill Street, Childers Qld 4660. Tel: (07) 4126 3711. Email: info@gruntlabour.com. Web: www.gruntlabour.com

Tourist Information. Tel: (07) 4126 1994.

Activities while you are there

Make the most of the historical aspects of the town by visiting the Childers Pharmaceutical Museum and the Olde Butcher Shoppe in addition to wandering around the historical streets. A visit to the Isis Central Mill from July to November allows you to see the sugar cane crushing process in action. Check with Tourist Information in the Palace Memorial Building in Churchill Street for details. Web: www.isisshire.info.

Chinchilla

Found on the Darling Downs about 300 km north west of Brisbane, Chinchilla is about a three-hour drive from Brisbane on the Warrego Highway. A town of nearly 4000, it is the service centre for the local region and is located close to Charleys Creek and the Condamine River. A long time centre for grain growing, recent agricultural developments include cotton farms, broad-acre farming, feedlots and energy industries.

Type of work

Melons dominate the horticultural scene in Chinchilla and provide work from November to April. Some 25 per cent of Australia's melons come from this region.

Approximate numbers

Several hundred are required for both rockmelons and watermelons.

Accommodation

There are a number of hotels and motels along with three caravan parks in town.

Transport

There are daily bus services to and from Brisbane.

Contacts

There is no employment agency in town placing people in seasonal jobs so phone the National Harvest Labour Information Service on 1800 062 332.

Tourist Information. Tel: (07) 4668 9564. Web: www.chinchilla.org.au

Activities while you are there

There are historical attractions around town including the well-regarded museum and the famous Boonarga Cactoblastis Hall which celebrates Chinchilla's role in the elimination of the prickly pear. If you have energy left after a solid weeks work you could go fossicking for the local famous petrified wood. If you have none, there is plenty of water you can swim in, boat on, or simply lay by. Otherwise there are drives around the local area including to the almost complete Kopan Creek power station which, when commissioned in late 2007 be one of the largest single unit generators in Australia and one of the cleanest as well. In February of every uneven year there is a Melon Festival celebrating one of the economic mainstays of the region.

Emerald

Established in 1879 the township suffered a number of fires during the early 1900s destroying many of the earlier buildings but sparing some which can be seen in their finery today. Found at the intersection of the Capricorn and Gregory highways it is some 270 km west of Rockhampton. With a population of around 10,000 in Emerald itself and a additional 18,000 in the surrounding towns and shires that together identify the region as the Central Highlands, there are plenty of things to do outside of work.

Type of work

Harvest trail work in this area centres mostly on cotton, melons, grapes and citrus crops. This means there is a spread of work throughout the year. It includes cotton chipping, picking and pruning.

Approximate numbers

Several hundred are required for each crop with the greatest number during the summer period.

Accommodation

There is a range of hotels and motels and a considerable number of caravan parks in the area. Backpacker accommodation is available but the development of coal mining in particular is putting pressure on accommodation prices. Use the website below to make contact with operators before you arrive.

Transport

There is a daily bus from Rockhampton and a weekly train service but out in this country you really need your own reliable vehicle.

Contacts

There is no employment agency in town placing people in seasonal jobs so phone the National Harvest Labour Information Service on 1800 062 332.

Tourist Information. Tel: (07) 4982 4142. Web: www.emeral.qld.gov.au

Activities while you are there

Emerald provides a clue as to its name as it nearby to the largest sapphire fields in the Southern Hemisphere. So if you are inclined, there is plenty of fossicking and digging that can be done on your time off. You do however, need a licence to do this and maps showing where you are allowed to dig. There are local historical sites and museums, a pleasant botanical garden but if you want to cool off then there is the Fairbairn Dam and Lake Maraboon.

Gatton

Located in the Lockyer Valley some 110 km west of Brisbane it is well known these days for Gatton College, now part of the University of Queensland, and reputed to be one of the best agricultural colleges in Australia. It was in this area that the earliest rural settlements in Queensland were established.

Type of work

The fertile black soils ensure there are vegetable crops year round, from those in the ground like potatoes, carrots, garlic and onions; those on the ground like lettuce, celery and cauliflower and those on vines like beans and peas.

Approximate numbers

Several hundred are required.

Accommodation

There are hotels and motels to chose from along with caravan parks. However, as the area is close to Brisbane and only 35 km from Toowoomba, there is a wider choice of accommodation including backpacker hostels. Woodstock Manor Hostel, in the nearby small town of Forest Hill (Tel: 07 5465 4453) has a good reputation as a workers hostel. Forest Hill is about 12 km from Gatton but closer to Laidley, also a centre for seasonal agricultural work.

Transport

Daily buses pass though from Brisbane to Toowoomba in addition to a regular train service.

Contacts

In addition to the Woodstock Manor Hostel phone the National Harvest Labour Information Service on 1800 062 332.

Tourist Information: Tel. (07) 5462 3430.

Activities while you are there

There are a number of historical sites in Gatton and nearby towns including the Gatton and District Historical Society Museum and it's possible to tour the agricultural college. Touring the nearby countryside by car is also an option as is taking a hot air balloon ride.

Gayndah

Gayndah was established in the 1840s, making it one of the oldest towns in the region. The area is renowned for its citrus industry and is a popular destination for backpackers.

Type of work

Easter until September/October is the main harvest time for citrus fruits including oranges, mandarines, grapefruit and lemons. There is however an opportunity to work in the orchards during the off-season from November to February doing thinning work.

Other opportunities exist in December and January for the grape harvest, although this is a much smaller industry than many other areas around Australia.

Approximate numbers

The citrus harvest requires 1500 to 2000 workers. Thinning and pruning in the off-season requires approximately 200 to 300 workers in the region while the grape harvest requires approximately 200 to 400 pickers, depending on the season.

Accommodation

Gayndah Riverview Caravan Park. Tel: (07) 4161 1280.

Transport

You will need your own transport.

Contacts

Harvest Trail Hotline. Tel: 1800 062 332

Citrus fruit growers

Benham M & A, 'Benyenda', Gayndah QLD 4625. Tel: (07) 4161 6177.

Glen Grove Orchard, Boomerang Road, Gayndah QLD 4625. Tel: (07) 4161 1196.

Glen Grove Orchard, 'Silverbush Shed', Gayndah QLD 4625. Tel: (07) 4161 1623.

Glenellen, Humphrey Binjour Road, Gayndah QLD 4625. Tel: (07) 4161 1955.

Golden Acres Citrus, 'Mt Lawless', Gayndah QLD 4625. Tel: (07) 4161 1532.

Riverton Orchard, Benyenda Road, Gayndah QLD 4625. Tel: (07) 4161 6173.

Robinson A G, Humphrey Binjour Road, Gayndah QLD 4625. Tel: (07) 4161 1955.

Smith L & M, 'Marlbec', Ideraway QLD 4625. Tel: (07) 4161 1630.

Two Pine Orchard, Bonaccord Road, Gayndah QLD 4625. Tel: (07) 4161 2285.

Whyte J & A, Mundubbera Road, Gayndah QLD 4625. Tel: (07) 4161 1845.

Activities while you are there

Swimming and fishing in the Burnett River, bird watching and visiting the Gayndah Museum. The Gayndah Orange Festival is staged every two years over the Queen's Birthday weekend in June.

Giru

Although Giru is small in size, the amount of work available in the region offers many opportunities. If you love mangoes, read on.

Type of work

The mango harvest is a short period between early November and Christmas during which work is on offer, and continuing through until January in the packing sheds.

Approximate numbers

During harvest between 1000 and 1500 workers are required for picking while a further 500 are needed in the packing sheds.

Accommodation

Mountain View Lake Holiday Park. Tel: (07) 4782 9122.

Transport

Daily bus services operate from Brisbane and Cairns.

Contacts

Burdekin Mango Growers Association, PO Box 2094, Ayr QLD 4807.

Tourist Information. Tel: (07) 4771 3061.

Fruit and berry growers

Farm Fresh Mangoes. Tel: (07) 4782 9529.

Kennedy I, Springwood Gardens, Mt Elliot Highway, Giru QLD 4809. Tel: 0427 719 271.

N.A.P. Townsville, Cnr Trembath Road & Bruce Highway, Horseshoe Lagoon QLD 4809. Tel: (07) 4782 9498.

Activities while you are there

Try your hand at Barramundi fishing or visit the Mount Elliot Bowling Green National Park.

Goondiwindi

Found at the intersection of the Newell, Barwon, Leichhardt, Gore, Cunningham and Bruxner highways just north of the NSW border, Goondiwindi boasts a large cotton growing industry with over 30,000 ha. The town has a population of around 5000 and is sited on the banks of the Macintrye River.

Type of work
There is a wide variety of agricultural production but the bulk of the work is in cotton chipping from November to January.

Approximate numbers
Several hundred.

Accommodation
There are a number of hotels, motels and caravan parks.

Transport
Coaches pass though on a regular basis.

Contacts
Best Employment: Tel. (07) 4671 4922. Toll free: 1800 660 660. Web: www.best.com.au

Tourist Information: Tel. (07) 4671 2653.

Activities while you are there
There are some local historical places including the Customs House Museum and the Cotton Gin, one of the largest in Australia, which runs tours during the cotton season. The river provides some quieter recreation and there is a 2 km walk along its banks. The local botanic garden is a popular location with its lake and lawns and 25 ha of native plants.

Gympie

Gympie has a population of 11,800 and is situated 161 km north of Brisbane. The town's name is derived from the Aboriginal word for a stinging nettle bush, which is found on the banks of the Mary River. Gold was discovered in 1867 and this attracted thousands of prospectors to the area. After around fifty years of gold fever, the rush was over and the town of Gympie then turned to dairy farming and the development of a strong horticultural industry.

Today Gympie is a tourist centre for the thousands of holiday makers who travel to the Sunshine Coast in search of relaxation. For many, a day trip to Gympie and the surrounding townships offers a contrast to the pristine beaches in the area, and an opportunity to explore some history by visiting the museums in town and to appreciate the countryside.

Type of work

Gympie offers the working traveller picking opportunities during various vegetable harvests, which begin in May and conclude around November. Crops in the area include beans, squash and cucumbers. Work in the area is very popular, mainly due to its proximity to the many attractions that surround the area, therefore it is recommended that you arrive in the area before harvest.

Approximate numbers

300 workers are required for the harvest period.

Accommodation

Gympie Caravan Park. Tel: (07) 5482 2382.

Transport

You will need your own transport.

Contacts

Tourist Information. Tel: (07) 5482 5444.

Fruit growers

Gold Glen Fruits, Bruce Highway, Glenwood QLD 4570. Tel: (07) 5485 7129.

Johnson E & E, 2 Happy Valley Road, Amamoor QLD 4570. Tel: (07) 5484 3130.

Kandanga Kreek, Riversdale Road, Kandanga QLD 4570. Tel: (07) 5484 3480.

McLellan Fruit Farms, Wolvi Road, Wolvi QLD 4570. Tel: (07) 5486 7375.

Sunfresh Pines, Tunnel Road, Kandanga QLD 4570. Tel: (07) 5484 5241.

Wilcox D & L, 4 Anderleigh Road, Kia Ora QLD 4570. Tel: (07) 5486 5139.

Yulebar, 11 Drummond Drive, Gympie QLD 4570. Tel: (07) 5482 4182.

Vegetable growers

P & N Dried Tomatoes, 2917 Old Gympie Road, Beerwah QLD 4519. Tel: (07) 5494 0900.

Paterson B & G, 55 Spanner Road, Glass House Mountains QLD 4518. Tel: (07) 5496 9178.

Suncoast Sprouts, 1144 Kin Kin-Pomona Road, Kin Kin QLD 4571. Tel: (07) 5485 4155.

Aquaculture

Cherax Park Aquaculture, Kanyan Road, Gunalda QLD 4570. Tel: (07) 5484 6096.

Eumundi Cray Fish, 1 Finley Road, Eumundi QLD 4562.
Tel: (07) 5442 7200.

Luxe Enterprises, Bribie Island Road, Ningi QLD 4511. Tel: (07) 5497 5755.

McHale Fisheries, 53 Hodgens Road, Peachester QLD 4519. Tel: (07) 5494 9712.

Noosa Crayfish Farms, 10 Capri Circuit, Noosa Heads QLD 4567. Tel: (07) 5449 2454.

Noosa Fish Farms, 44 Pine Street, Cooroy QLD 4563. Tel: (07) 5442 5629.

Sunland Freshwater Fish Hatchery, Gilson Road, Boreen Point QLD 4565. Tel: (07) 5485 3144.

Sunshine Coast Cray & Fish Producers, RMS 1197, Yandina QLD 4561. Tel: (07) 5446 6319.

Activities while you are there

The Goldrush Festival is held every October while the Gympie

Country Music Festival attracts many people into the town in August creating a real party atmosphere.

Innisfail

Located 90 km south of Cairns, Innisfail is an interesting place to visit. After World War I, a large influx of mainly Italian immigrants came to the area, adding a cosmopolitan feel to the town. The friendly town has a very busy fishing port, home to prawn trawlers and mackerel boats, which rest between trips in the Johnstone River.

Type of work

Apart from occasional work that can be found on fishing trawlers and line-fishing boats, Innisfail has a healthy banana industry, which creates employment opportunities from May until December to January.

Approximate numbers

Between 400 and 600 workers are required for the banana plantations.

Accommodation

Backpackers Innisfail, 73 Rankin Street, Innisfail Qld 4860.

Flying Fish Point Caravan Park. Tel: (07) 4061 3131.

River Drive Van Park. Tel: (07) 4061 2515.

Transport

Train and bus services operate from Brisbane and Cairns.

Contacts

Tourist Information. Tel: (07) 4061 6448.

Banana growers

Borsato R & K, Lot 2 Bruce Highway, Innisfail QLD 4860. Tel: (07) 4061 6264.

Chiquita North Queensland, Jubilee Road, Innisfail QLD 4860. Tel: (07) 4063 3933.

Hampson Bros, Palmerston Highway, East Palmerston QLD 4860. Tel: (07) 4064 5282.

Marcelport, Dinner Creek Road, Garradunga QLD 4860. Tel: (07) 4063 3852.

Pacific Coast Produce, 228 Boogan Road, Innisfail QLD 4860. Tel: (07) 4064 2452.

Spagspac, Bertei Road, Pin Gin Hill QLD 4860. Tel: (07) 4064 4137.

Vick S & H, Palmerston Highway, Pin Gin Hill QLD 4860. Tel: (07) 4064 4167.

Vue Y, Gattera Road, Nerada QLD 4860. Tel: (07) 4064 5210.

Warraker Creek Quality Bananas, Warraker Creek Road, Upper Daradgee QLD 4860. Tel: (07) 4063 3661.

Zecchinati Plantation, Pullom Road, East Palmerston QLD 4860. Tel: (07) 4064 5171.

Activities while you are there

If you are interested in bushwalking, take the track up Mt Bartle Frere, it is Queensland's highest mountain and is located just north of the town. For a gentle sightsee, try Paronella Park, where you'll find a Spanish-style castle built by a migrant called (you guessed it!) Jose Paronella.

Mundubbera

Mundubbera is located 363 km from Brisbane and has a population of 2300. Known as the citrus centre of Queensland, Mundubbera's claim to fame is their giant mandarine, which also acts as an information centre for the town, as well as the seasonal harvest office.

Type of work

Work is available for the citrus harvest from April through until late October. The area offers a timely opportunity for the working traveller who has spent previous months down south or in Western Australia picking for the grape harvest with many pickers required during the season.

Approximate numbers

Over 1000 workers are required for the harvest season between April and October.

Accommodation

Citrus Country Caravan Village. Tel: (07) 4165 4549.

Mundubbera Caravan Park. Tel: (07) 4165 4549.

Transport

Your own transport would be helpful to get to work areas however, bus services operate to and from Brisbane.

Contacts

Citrus fruit growers

Auburnvale Citrus, Hawkwood Road, Derri Derra QLD 4626. Tel: (07) 4165 6134.

Golden Mile Orchards, 2 Durong Road, Mundubbera QLD 4626. Tel: (07) 4165 4555.

Quebec Orchard, Mundubbera QLD 4626. Tel: (07) 4165 6139.

Trott B & J & Son, Coonambula Road, Mundubbera QLD 4626. Tel: (07) 4165 4755.

Zipf N & Sons, Glenrae Dip Road, Mundubbera QLD 4626. Tel: (07) 4165 4377.

Activities while you are there

Mundubbera is located where the Boyne, Auburn and Burnett rivers intersect and therefore offers many water sport activities, as well as horse riding and bushwalking in the Auburn River National Park.

Nambour

Nambour is less than 100 km north of Brisbane and is surrounded by sugar plantations. The town and nearby areas have a population of around 22,700 and the area is going through a major population spurt based in part on a growing tourism industry which is growing given its proximity to Brisbane.

Type of work

Known for its sugar, Nambour also has a strong strawberry industry, with harvest taking place between August and November. The Sunshine Plantation south of Nambour which is marked by a giant pineapple, grows a variety of tropical fruits and spices.

Approximate numbers

Between 300 and 600 workers are required for the strawberry harvest.

Accommodation

Cotton Tree Beach House, 15 The Esplanade, Maroochydore QLD 4558. Tel: (07) 5443 1755.

Maroochydore YHA Holiday Hostel Backpackers, 24 Schirrman Drive, Maroochydore QLD 4558. Tel: (07) 5443 3151.

Nambour Rainforest Holiday Cabin Village. Tel: (07) 5442 1153.

Nearby Maroochydore has the following accommodation:

Suncoast Backpackers Lodge, 50 Parker Street, Maroochydore QLD 4558. Tel: (07) 5443 7544.

Transport

A daily bus service operates from Brisbane.

Contacts

Sunlands Market Farmers Co-Operative Association, Fruithau 1 Building, 12 Concorde Place, Caboolture Corporate Park, Caboolture QLD 4510. Tel: 0412 070 005

Tourist Information. Tel: (07) 5443 6400.

Fruit and berry growers

Allandale Pines, Spanner Road, Glass House Mountains QLD 4518. Tel: (07) 5493 0666.

Berry Patch Marketing, Lot 1 O'Shea Road, Wamuran QLD 4512. Tel: (07) 5496 6880.

Diamond Valley Mangoes, 385 Diamondfield Road, Amamoor QLD 4570. Tel: (07) 5484 3335.

Eumundi Strawberry Farm, Strawberry Lane, Eumundi QLD 4562. Tel: (07) 5442 8213.

Forest Hill Fruits, Mapleton Road, Nambour QLD 4560. Tel: (07) 5441 7299.

Forster R & R, 160 Judds Road, Glass House Mountains QLD 4518. Tel: (07) 5496 9129.

Johnson E & E, 2 Happy Valley Road, Amamoor QLD 4570. Tel: (07) 5484 3130.

Kandanga Kreek, Riversdale Road, Kandanga QLD 4570. Tel: (07) 5484 3480.

Lankester Avocados, Winston Road, Palmwoods QLD 4555. Tel: (07) 5445 9922.

McLellan Fruit Farms, Wolvi Road, Wolvi QLD 4570. Tel: (07) 5486 7375.

Moffat C & M, 9 Georgina Place, Beerwah QLD 4519. Tel: (07) 5494 0593.

Rohlf Strawberries, 1 Derek Road, Wamuran QLD 4512. Tel: (07) 5496 6477.

Schiffke, 210 Stern Road, Bellmere QLD 4510. Tel: (07) 5495 8274.

Sippy Orchards, Wilson Road, Eudlo QLD 4554. Tel: (07) 5445 9499.

Somerset Springs, 1358 Mount Kilcoy Road, Kilcoy QLD 4515. Tel: (07) 5498 1252.

Strawberry Fields, 133 Laxton Road, Palmview QLD 4553. Tel: (07) 5494 5146.

Sunfresh Pines, Tunnel Road, Kandanga QLD 4570. Tel: (07) 5484 5241.

Wilcox D & L, 4 Anderleigh Road, Kia Ora QLD 4570. Tel: (07) 5486 5139.

Vineyards

Blind Man's Bluff Vineyards, Lot 15 Wilcox & Bluff Roads, Kenilworth QLD 4574. Tel: (07) 5472 3168.

Dingo Creek Vineyard, 265 Tandur-Traveston Road, Traveston QLD 4570. Tel: (07) 5485 1731.

Eumundi Winery, 310 Memorial Drive, Eumundi QLD 4562. Tel: (07) 5442 7444.

Flaxton Grove Vineyard & Cellars, Main Road, Flaxton QLD 4560. Tel: (07) 5478 6555.

Flaxton Grove Winery, 313 Flaxton Drive, Flaxton QLD 4560. Tel: (07) 5478 6766.

Glengariff (Historic) Estate – Winery & Vineyard, 3234 Mt Mee Road, Dayboro QLD 4521. Tel: (07) 3425 1299.

Hunting Lodge Estate Winery & African Cabins, 703 Mt Kilcoy Road, Mt Kilcoy QLD 4515. Tel: (07) 5498 1243.

Kenilworth Bluff Winery, Lot 13 Bluff Road, Kenilworth QLD 4574. Tel: (07) 5472 3723.

Kenilworth Bluff Wines, Bluff Road, Kenilworth QLD 4574. Tel: (07) 5472 3723.

Little Morgue Winery, Nambour-Yandina Connection Road, Yandina QLD 4561. Tel: (07) 5441 5951.

Maleny Mountain Wines, 787 Landsborough Maleny Road, Maleny QLD 4552. Tel: (07) 5429 6300.

Robinsons Family Vineyards, 855 Noosa Eumundi Road, Doonan QLD 4562. Tel: (07) 5471 1129.

Settlers Rise-Montville Vineyard & Winery, 249 Western Avenue, Montville QLD 4560. Tel: (07) 5478 5558.

7 Acres Winery, 374 Mons Road, Forest Glen QLD 4556. Tel: (07) 5445 1198.

Sweet Water Hill Wines, 17 Roberts Road, Anderleigh QLD 4570. Tel: (07) 5485 7007.

Activities while you are there

Visit some of the local attractions including the Big Pineapple, Bribie Island and Underwater World. The area is located near the Sunshine Coast and therefore has a lot to offer by way of recreation and relaxation.

Stanthorpe

The town of Stanthorpe is located 219 km south-west of Brisbane at an elevation of 811 m above sea level, making it one of the highest towns in Queensland. Due to the cooler climate, Stanthorpe is a great place to visit on hot days, but equally, it has the perfect climate for stone fruit and other cooler climate produce and is therefore a very popular destination for working travellers.

Type of work

A great variety of produce is grown in the Stanthorpe region. Vegetable crops including tomatoes and lettuce are harvested between January and April. The grape harvest follows a similar trend.

Stone fruits, including peaches and nectarines, have a shorter harvest period during January and February and there is a fair amount of competition from locals and other travellers for work, so ensure you arrive in the area just before harvest time to maximise your opportunities.

Approximate numbers

From January to April over 3000 workers are required for the harvest.

Accommodation

The Summit Backpackers Hostel. Tel: (07) 4683 2599.

Top of the Town Caravan Park. Tel: (07) 4681 2030.

Transport

A daily bus service operates from Brisbane.

Contacts

Best Employment, 19 Victoria Street, Stanthorpe QLD 4380. Tel: (07) 4681 2022.

Employment National, Stanthorpe Harvest Office, Cnr Railway & Rogers Streets, Stanthorpe QLD 4380. Tel: 1300 720 126.

Tourist Information. Tel: (07) 4681 2057.

Fruit and berry growers

Barbierato L & J, 'Mt You You Orchard', Pikedale QLD 4380. Tel: (07) 4685 6168.

Harvey W & A, 'Vamanha', Eukey QLD 4380. Tel: (07) 4683 7156.

Pugno P & P, MS 649, Eukey via Stanthorpe QLD 4380. Tel: (07) 4683 7154.

Vegetable growers

Gasparin A & Sons, Gentle Road, Stanthorpe QLD 4380. Tel: (07) 4681 2175.

Girardi Farms, West Road, Stanthorpe QLD 4380. Tel: (07) 4681 2238.

Red Rosella, Mt Tully Road, Stanthorpe QLD 4380. Tel: (07) 4681 1383.

Activities while you are there

Within a short distance of Stanthorpe you will find the beautiful Girraween National Park. In addition, there are wineries to visit and if you are in the area during October, join in the festivities at the Granite Belt Spring Wine Festival.

St George

Some 550 km west of Brisbane, St George has its unexpected name because Sir Thomas Mitchell crossed the Balonne River here on St George's Day (23 April) in 1846. Now with a population of around 3800, St George is the centre of a rich agricultural area with beef, sheep, grain, horticultural crops and cotton. The necessary water for irrigation comes from artesian water and the Beardmore Dam. The irrigated area is just south of the town and covers some 13,00 ha.

Type of work

Almost all seasonal employment is centred on the horticultural and cotton farms with picking and chipping work.

Approximate numbers

Several hundred.

Accommodation

There are several hotels, motels and caravan parks in the town.

Transport

When you are this far west, you really need your own transport.

Contacts

Best Employment: Tel. (07) 4671 4922. Toll free: 1800 660 660. Web: www.best.com.au.

Tourist Information: Tel: (07) 4620 8877.

Activities while you are there

In town there is a substantial display of carved emu eggs that has been on the World Expo circuit, a heritage centre and a number of historical buildings. Those keen on fishing can put the claim of good fishing in the local rivers and creeks to the test. The Rosehill Aviaries Wildlife Park to the west of St George has some 80 aviaries with 600 birds representing 70 species while there are a number of local examples of ancient rock wells carved out of the rock by Aborigines thousands of years ago. Beardmore Dam provides a place for watersports.

Tully

Tully has a population of 3100 and is located just south of Innisfail. Due to its proximity to Cairns, Tully and surrounding areas have easy access to a busy large town, yet are set among beautiful rainforests and banana plantations! Tully is also one of the favourite destinations of international backpackers for work and play, with fantastic white-water rafting on the Tully River. Each year the local sugar mill crushes 1.8 million tonnes of sugar cane and 8.5 million boxes of bananas are sent out of the area (cyclone years excepted), so plenty of seasonal workers are required.

Type of work

The banana industry requires workers all year round for picking, planting and general maintenance of the many plantations in the area.

Approximate numbers

Numbers required fluctuate, depending on the month, but with patience and a smile, your best bet is direct gate calling. As a rough guide, at any one time the banana plantations in the area need 50 to 150 workers.

Accommodation

Googarra Caravan Park. Tel: (07) 4066 9325.

Tully Head Van Park. Tel: (07) 4066 9260.

Transport

Tully is connected to surrounding areas by train and bus services. Many growers in the area have banded together to make it attractive for working travellers by offering a worker's pick-up point in town first thing in the morning and a drop-off point in the afternoon.

Contacts

Tourist Information: Tel: (07) 4061 6448.

Banana growers

AG White, Tea Plantation Road, Tully QLD 4854. Tel: (07) 4068 2883.

Banana Growers' Liaison Officer, Midtown Shopping Plaza, Tully QLD 4854. Tel: (07) 4068 2255.

Chiquita North Queensland, Mullins Road, Tully QLD 4854. Tel: (07) 4066 7764.

Clifford M & J, Russell Henry Road, Murray Upper QLD 4854. Tel: (07) 4066 5571.

Collins L, 8 Bamber Street, Tully QLD 4854. Tel: (07) 4068 1268.

Dores Bananas, Dores Road, Murray Upper QLD 4854. Tel: (07) 4066 5561.

Dundee Creek Banana Co., Bruce Highway, Tully QLD 4854. Tel: (07) 4068 2770.

Gilbert P & Sons, 761 Syndicate Road, Tully QLD 4854. Tel: (07) 4066 7720.

Johnston M & J, Davidson Road, Euramo QLD 4854. Tel: (07) 4066 7862.

Kent P, Murray Falls Road, Murray Upper QLD 4854. Tel: (07) 4066 5594.

Lissio M, Mullins Road, Tully QLD 4854. Tel: (07) 4066 7980.

MJ Bananas, Riversdale Road, Euramo QLD 4854. Tel: (07) 4066 7846.

Murray Falls Plantation, Murray Falls Road, Murray Upper QLD 4854. Tel: (07) 4066 5548.

NQ Banana Growers Co-op Association, Tips Building, Bruce Highway, Tully QLD 4854. Tel: (07) 4068 3300.

Oberthur, L, Lot 5 Davidson Road, Euramo QLD 4854. Tel: (07) 4066 7865.

Queensland Fruit & Vegetable Growers Banana Liaison Officer, Midtown Shopping Plaza, Tully QLD 4854. Tel: (07) 4068 2255.

Ugana Plantation, Nicotra Road, Tully QLD 4854. Tel: (07) 4068 2761.

Activities while you are there

Between June and December try a visit to the Tully Sugar Mill and definitely give the white-water rafting a go!

Harvest trail - New South Wales

Barham

Barham is a small town on the Murray River about 825 km south-west of Sydney. Main activities are timber and agriculture. It's just over the border from Kerang in Victoria.

Type of work

For the travelling worker, Barham can offer citrus fruit and tomato picking during the summer months.

Approximate numbers

Farmers look for seasonal workers from mid December, with the peak of the picking season being late January through to February.

Accommodation

Barham Lakes Caravan Park, East Barham Road, Barham NSW 2732. Tel: (03) 5453 2009.

Transport

Coming from Melbourne, head along the Loddon Valley Highway until you reach Kerang, then turn off to Barham, which is 28 km north-east and over the Murray River. You'll need a car to get to town.

Contacts

There is no tourist information centre in town.

Fruit growers

Kurrnung Estate, Barham NSW 2732. Tel: (03) 5453 2177.

Selleck RB & DG, Barham NSW 2732. Tel: (03) 5453 2329.

Activities while you are there

Activities include swimming, fishing, wind-surfing, water skiing and some great bush walks.

Bathurst

Bathurst was founded in 1815 and is Australia's oldest inland city, nestled among rolling hills and the Macquarie River. With a population in excess of 30,000 people, Bathurst is a sizeable and very well established city, which attracts travellers from far and wide, especially during October for the Mount Panorama car race, that can provide the working traveller with employment opportunities particularly in hospitality.

Type of work

Bathurst is a large enough city to offer casual work opportunities all year round if you are prepared to look for them. As mentioned above, during October, motorcar enthusiasts flock to see one of the main racing events on the calendar. This obviously brings short-term employment opportunities to the area and with some experience in the hospitality industry you should find work in general catering, bar work or waiting. A month prior to the car racing event, work is also needed in the form of manual labour to assist in building spectator stands and food stalls. The Bathurst region has a modest stone fruit and apple industry, where work is available from November to February. Before Christmas, the main work is involved in thinning crops, with the main picking season after Christmas and running as late as March.

Approximate numbers

Up to 500 pickers are required during the peak months. Over 200 are required for the Mt Panorama car racing event.

Accommodation

Bathurst Caravan Park. Tel: (02) 6331 8286.

Transport

Bathurst is serviced by the XPT train daily from Sydney; call 132 232 for pricing and schedules. By road, Bathurst is situated 240 km west of Sydney and is reached by the Great Western Highway.

Contacts

Tourist Information: Tel: (02) 6333 6288.

Fruit and berry growers

Appledore Orchard, O'Connell Road, Bathurst NSW 2795. Tel: (02) 6331 7618.

Rayner H, College Road, Bathurst NSW 2795. Tel: (02) 6331 4387.

Activities while you are there

The Macquarie River offers a number of water sport activities including canoeing and fishing. The town also has a long history, with many buildings and landmarks to visit in the town and around the region.

Batlow

Batlow is located some 467 km south-west of Sydney and north-west of the Kosciuszko National Park, and has a population of 1270. The town's name was originally Reedy Flat, named after the surveyor who planned the town. Historically, Batlow lived and breathed the gold rush, but today is home to a thriving apple and pear industry.

Type of work

As mentioned, apples and pears are the main crop around the area and there is plenty of pruning and picking work, which can run from December right through to May. In addition to apples and pears, Batlow has a large stone fruit industry, which requires workers over the harvest period from November to April. Hourly rates for picking are around the $12.50 mark and with 80+ orchards around the area, there is plenty of work available during peak times. First stop is the local caravan park to discuss where work is available and on-site caravan accommodation starts at around $128.00 per week. Tent fees (un-powered site) are around $36.00 per week.

Approximate numbers

Up to 2000 pickers are required during the harvest and around 200 pruners in the off-season, although numbers can vary greatly depending on the quality of the season.

Accommodation

Batlow Caravan Park. Tel: (02) 6949 1444.

Batlow Hotel. Tel: (02) 6949 1001.

Transport

Own car required.

Contacts

Bowden J & B & Sons, Old Tumbarumba Road, Batlow NSW 2750. Tel: (02) 6949 1771.

Tourist Information. Tel: (02) 6947 1849.

Blueberry growers

Tumbarumba Blueberries (www.tumbaberry.com.au), 134 Taradale Road, Tumbarumba NSW 2653. Tel: (02) 69482841

Tumbarumba Blueberry Producers was established to capitalise on the geographic location of the Tumbarumba region. Blueberries were first planted here in 1983 and most of the original plants are still in the ground. New plantings have taken Tumbarumba Blueberries to 36 hectares on two farms, both within eight kilometres of town.

A large labour force is required in the harvest season when up to 250 people are employed. The blueberry season runs from late December to early February. Fruit is often picked, packed, cooled and shipped on the same day.

Apple growers

Bowden S, 'Fruits of Batlow', 1 Cottams Road, Batlow NSW 2730. Tel: (02) 6949 1835.

Dodds L & B, 'Greenlands', Batlow NSW 2730. Tel: (02) 6949 1761.

Eccleston J & J, 39 Cemetery Road, Batlow NSW 2730. Tel: (02) 6949 1466.

Mount View Orchards Batlow, Old Tumbarumba Road, Batlow NSW 2730. Tel: (02) 6949 1765.

Nightingale Bros, 706a Greenhills Forest Road, Batlow NSW 2730. Tel: (02) 6949 1491.

Springfields Orchards, Tumut Road, Batlow NSW 2730. Tel: (02) 6949 1021.

Fruit and berry growers

Ardrossan Nurseries, Old Tumbarumba Road, Batlow NSW 2730. Tel: (02) 6949 1710.

Ashton D, 'Dundee', Batlow NSW 2730. Tel: (02) 6949 1654.

Cremorne Brothers Orchards, 'Sunningdale Park', Batlow NSW 2730. Tel: (02) 6949 1745.

Faulkner J, 'Haroldene', Batlow NSW 2730. Tel: (02) 6949 1087.

Gilbert I & M, Belmont Orchards, Batlow NSW 2730. Tel: 0412 564 411.

Heatley R & J, Packing Shed, Batlow NSW 2730. Tel: (02) 6949 1194.

Sedgewick R, Tumbarumba Road, Batlow NSW 2730. Tel: (02) 6949 1046.

Vanzella Adrian A, 'The Springs', Batlow NSW 2730. Tel: (02) 6949 1137.

Activities while you are there

Batlow is very close to Lake Blowering, which is part of the irrigation system for Batlow and surrounding towns. The town is also in close proximity to the mountains, so depending on what time of year you visit, Batlow and the area offer a diverse range of activities, including fishing, water sports, bushwalking, skiing and many others.

Bourke

Bourke represents the outback in New South Wales shown by the saying 'Back O'Bourke', implying a place of extreme outback remoteness. Indeed, one could argue that Bourke is the beginning of a new world, a real Australia that city-slickers have only read about in the verse of Henry Lawson and other great Australian poets.

Bourke was once a bustling town where wool from the great sheep stations was shipped down the Darling River, the lifeblood of Bourke. Today, the same waterway infuses the land surrounding Bourke with fields irrigated from the Darling River, making for an agricultural industry and casual/seasonal work for travellers.

Type of work

There is diversity in the produce grown in and around Bourke. Cotton is the main crop grown in the region, although various other crops including grapes, stone fruits and citrus fruits are all on the increase. With a population of little over 3000, and some great watering holes (hotels) for a beer and chat with the locals, you are sure to find some work via a reliable source in the public bar in the late afternoon!

Approximate numbers

Around 700 to 1000 cotton chippers are needed from April to May and 300 to 400 workers are required for the grape harvest from December to early February. The stone fruit harvest from November to December requires about 300 workers.

Accommodation

Mitchell Caravan Park. Tel: (02) 6872 2791.

Paddlewheel Caravan Park. Tel: (02) 6872 2277.

Transport

From Sydney catch the train to Dubbo, then a bus to Bourke.

Contacts

Back O'Bourke Fruits, Hungerford Road, Bourke NSW 2840. Tel: (02) 6872 1888.

Darling Farms, Wanaaring Road, Bourke NSW 2840. Tel: (02) 6872 2833.

OEC Employment, 30 Oxley Street, Bourke NSW 2840. Tel: 1800 065 188.

Citrus growers

Pitches R & G, Hindbury North, Bourke NSW 2840. Tel: (02) 6872 2267.

Activities while you are there

The Darling River offers fishing and swimming. There are also a number of festivals throughout the year including the Bourke Mateship festival in September, which includes among other things a fantastic exhibition of Bourke's history. The major rodeo on the calendar is the Back O'Bourke Stampede held in October.

Cessnock

In heart of the Hunter Valley wine region, Cessnock is a destination for many local and overseas visitors attracted by the booming wine industry and associated services. With over 70 vineyards in the local area its proximity to Sydney—only 160 kms—makes Cessnock a perfect day trip for all but the designated driver! For those looking at making the most of the area by spending a few days in the region, there is plenty of accommodation.

Type of work

Although Cessnock and surrounding areas has a relatively high unemployment rate, there is both longer term and seasonal work available for experienced chefs, bar workers and wait staff, particularly in the five-star establishments. Be sure to take references with you when applying for jobs in the hospitality trade. Christmas and school holidays are very busy in the region, while during the winter months, families and couples tend to flock to the Hunter region for weekends, which can offer the worker some consistency for longer periods.

Vacancies in the vineyards peak during January to March, but make sure you're in the area around Christmas time or just after, to increase your chances of work. During the winter months, people are required to prune and maintain the vines.

Approximate numbers

The hospitality industry requires 200+ workers but this can be quite seasonal.

During harvest time more than 800 seasonal workers are required for about two months beginning in January. Up to 150 'off season' workers are required to maintain vines in the cooler months.

Accommodation

The area has many caravan parks that allow long term stay.

Transport

Cessnock is easily reached from both Sydney and Newcastle with daily buses to the area. For those driving from Sydney, allow a couple of hours to get to your destination.

Contacts

Vineyards

Wesley Uniting Employment, 5 Edward Street, Cessnock NSW 2325. Tel: (02) 4993 3200.

Vegetable growers

Beavan R, Combo Lane, Singleton NSW 2330. Tel: (02) 6572 4189.

Sciberras Produce, George Down Drive, Kulnura NSW 2250. Tel: (02) 4376 1011.

Fruit growers

Tull Kevin, 225 Mathieson Street, Bellbird NSW 2325. Tel: (02) 4990 4974.

Coffs Harbour

With a population of around 60,000 Coffs is substantial town 560 km north of Sydney. It is a significant tourism town year round both because of the town itself and nearby attractions including the Bellingen Valley. It also well known for its bananas with the Big Banana above the highway at Coffs being one of the first 'big things' in Australia. In recent years there has been a growth in the blueberry industry in the region based at Corindi, some 40 km north of Coffs.

Type of work

Work in the banana industry around Coffs is not as readily available as it is around Tully in North Queensland and so fewer people are required on a seasonal basis. The blueberry farms however, require a considerable number at picking time. In addition there are a number of other crops requiring picking though with smaller numbers.

Approximate numbers

Several hundred are needed for blueberry picking in Corindi. Blueberry Farms of Australia with the largest blueberry farms in Australia is now owned by Costa Exchange, see www.costaexchange.com.au.

Accommodation

There are many hotels and motels in the area but the caravan parks and backpackers hostels in the area are more appropriate given the cost of the former. The cost of accommodation rises significantly during the school holidays. Some of the backpacker hostels are able to provide information about work in the area. Barracuda Backpackers (Tel. 02 6651 3514) is one such hostel.

Transport

Coaches travelling between Sydney and Brisbane pass through the town daily. A train is also available but a car is very useful for local travel to farms and outlying areas.

Contacts

Blueberry Farms of Australia: (02) 6649 2921, 6649 2861. You need to make arrangements before arriving in the area.

Tourist Information: (02) 6652 1522, 1800 025 650.

Activities while you are there

As the area is a major regional tourist centre there are many things to do and see. Being on the beach there is surfing, paddling or just sunning yourself. There are a number of dive schools for those who would like to try. The botanical garden is worth a visit and further out of town there are trips to rainforests and rafting down rivers.

Cowra

Cowra is 307 km west of Sydney with a population of 8500. The town's name comes from the Aboriginal word meaning 'rocks', which makes sense as large granite rocks surround the township. The main produce in and around Cowra includes lambs, cattle, wool, asparagus and other vegetables.

At the end of the Second World War, Cowra housed over 3000 European immigrants from countries including Poland, Latvia and Estonia. Some of the men worked on the now famous Snowy Mountains Scheme, while the women worked the land and cared for their children. In 1944 there was a breakout from the prisoner-of-war camp near the town in which four Australian guards were killed and 230 Japanese soldiers died. Some 380 prisoners escaped and it took nine days to recapture all those who broke out. Interestingly, the town now celebrates several Japanese festivals and is home to the beautiful Japanese Garden designed by Ken Nakajima, which are similar to the Imperial Gardens in Kyoto, Japan.

Type of work

Vineyards are developing in the area and therefore offering more and more work opportunities during the grape harvest, which is February to April. Much of this grape harvest is sent to wineries outside of the area for processing.

Cowra is also known for its asparagus and tomatoes, with a large export market developed by Cowra Export Packers. Asparagus cutters must be highly experienced and therefore this type of work is not really available to the average travelling worker. In fact, many of the asparagus cutters come from overseas to cut the harvest each season. However, packing work is available at the end of November.

Approximate numbers

200 to 300 workers are needed for the grape harvest and up to 150 workers in the packing sheds for asparagus.

Accommodation

Caravan City Holiday Resort. Tel: (019) 659 333.

Pine Trees Caravan Park. Tel: (02) 6542 1850.

Transport

Your own transport is required.

Contacts

Cowra Export Packers employ casual and seasonal workers for packing work during the periods of February until the end of March for tomatoes and September until the end of November for asparagus. Hourly rates for packing are approximately $13 per hour and those interested must apply in person. Cowra Export Packers Co-operative, North Logan Road, Cowra NSW 2794. Tel: (02) 6342 1576.

Tourist Information. Tel: (02) 6342 4333.

Apple and pear growers

Armstrong R J, 'Doocarrick' Nashdale NSW 2800. Tel: (02) 6365 3104.

Carthew B, Towac Road, Canobolas NSW 2800. Tel: (02) 6365 3138.

Carthew G D, Pinnacle Road, Orange NSW 2800. Tel: (02) 6365 3231.

Cunial A & D, 'Carinya' Nashdale NSW 2800. Tel: (02) 6365 3172.

Darley P & D, 'Daydawn' Nashdale NSW 2800. Tel: (02) 6365 3278.

Emmi G & M, 30 Canobolas Road, Orange NSW 2800. Tel: (02) 6365 3326.

Gartrell D & C, 'Wattleview' Mt Lofty Road, Nashdale NSW 2800. Tel: (02) 6365 3233.

Gottschall C, 21 Cadia Road, Orange NSW 2800. Tel: (02) 6362 4647.

Hawke D, Lysterfield Road, Orange NSW 2800. Tel: (02) 6365 3109.

Kirkwood J, 'Ballykeane', Orange NSW 2800. Tel: (02) 6362 9960.

Kirkwood J, Stoneleigh Orchard, Orange NSW 2800. Tel: (02) 6365 8231.

McClymont P A, Springside NSW 2800. Tel: (02) 6365 4308.

McClymont R & J, 'Winfield', Springside NSW 2800. Tel: (02) 6365 4261.

Pearce R, 'Mirrabooka', Orange NSW 2800. Tel: (02) 6365 8216.

Perry K, 'Sunny Crest', Orange NSW 2800. Tel: (02) 6365 3239.

Previtera P & G, 63 Pinnacle Road, Orange NSW 2800. Tel: (02) 6365 3300.

Prudhomme P & A, 'Ku-Ring-Gai', Nashdale NSW 2800. Tel: (02) 6365 3289.

Rossetto Orchards, Ploughmans Lane, Orange NSW 2800. Tel: (02) 6361 4545.

Vardanega D & J, 40 Pinnacle Road, Orange NSW 2800. Tel: (02) 6365 3242.

Vardanega M, Cargo Road, Orange NSW 2800. Tel: (02) 6361 4549.

Vineyards

Chiveton, 605 Grenfell Road, Cowra NSW 2794. Tel: (02) 6342 9270.

Cowra Wines, Boorowa Road, Cowra NSW 2794. Tel: (02) 6342 1136.

Kalari Vineyards, Carro Park Road, Cowra NSW 2794. Tel: (02) 6342 1465.

Kiola Vineyard Services, 9 Delaneys Road, Cowra NSW 2794. Tel: 0429 639 839.

Richmond Grove Cowra, Reids Flat Road, Cowra NSW 2794. Tel: (02) 6341 1088.

The Mill Winery, 6 Vaux Street, Cowra NSW 2794. Tel: (02) 6341 4141.

Activities while you are there

Check out Australia's World Peace Bell, which is a replica of the one in the United Nations building in New York City. Other activities include bird watching, stargazing, water sports and bushwalking. In the month of April, join in with the Moon Gazing Night at the well-known Japanese Gardens or visit Darby Falls Observatory.

Festivals include Cowra Picnic Races and Wine Show in July, the Cowra Agricultural Show in September and the Sakura and Matsuri Festivals in October, which include martial arts, pottery and calligraphy demonstrations.

Forbes

Forbes is situated near the banks of the Lachlan River, 371 km west of Sydney. The town is of historical importance, having experienced a gold rush in the mid 1800s, which saw the town grow as huge numbers of prospectors arrived seeking their fame and fortune.

Forbes has stood the test of time and today is a thriving town with a large fruit and vegetable industry, making it a very popular stopover for the working traveller. The area has also increased its grape production in recent times.

Type of work

The apple and pear harvest takes place from November and concludes in late March. Each year there is a strong demand for pickers to cover the harvest. Forbes is also known for its large tomato crop and again pickers are required in January and can expect work right through to the end of March. Asparagus is also grown in the area for both the domestic and export markets although you will need to be experienced in cutting the produce to obtain this type of work.

Approximate numbers

In total, approximately 80 to 100 workers are required to cover both the apple, pear and tomato harvests, while further work can be sought during the winter months for pruning and general orchard maintenance.

Accommodation

Apex Caravan Park. Tel: (02) 6852 1929.

Lachlan View Caravan Park. Tel: (02) 6852 1055.

Transport

Daily bus service from Sydney.

Contacts

Forbes Employment Service, 100 Rankin Street, Forbes NSW 2871. Tel: (02) 6851 6966.

Sunnyside Orchard Packing Shed, Gilgandra Road Dubbo NSW 2830. Tel: 0412 416 058.

Tourist Information. Tel: (02) 6851 1288.

Fruit and berry growers

Betland B & M, 'Dilga', Bundaburrah NSW 2871. Tel: (02) 6853 2240.

Ellison R, South Lead Road, Forbes NSW 2871. Tel: (02) 6852 1704.

Girot N, 'French Park', Forbes NSW 2871. Tel: (02) 6852 1226.

Mark wort F, South Condobolin Road, Forbes NSW 2871. Tel: (02) 6852 1952.

Parkview Orchards, Off Show Street, Forbes NSW 2871. Tel: (02) 6851 2624.

Activities while you are there

Check out the Lachlan Vintage Village, which is a reconstruction of the town during the 1800s. Drive down to the Gum Swamp, a bird watchers' hide overlooking the swamp. If you like jazz, head to Forbes in January for the annual Jazz Festival. You can also partake in wine tasting at Sandhills Vineyard and Lachlan Valley Wines.

Griffith

Griffith is located six hours west of Sydney and five and a half hours north-west of Melbourne, in the heart of the rich agricultural lands of the Riverina. Harvest work is available year round, depending on climatic conditions, crop size and quality. Crops grown in the district include oranges, mandarines, grapes, stone fruits and onions. The demand for workers usually peaks between November and March.

Transport to Griffith is well established, with services available from all capital cities operated by Countrylink rail services and Greyhound Australia coaches. Most orchards are located within a 20 km radius of the town, however taxis are the only form of public transport, so it helps if you have your own transport.

There are a number of hotels and motels in the town, but during the peak season demand for rooms is high and booking is essential. Local caravan parks also have excellent facilities, including camping grounds. Bringing your own camping gear is highly recommended.

Type of work

The Riverina area, irrigated by the Murrumbidgee River, is the perfect place for the working traveller to settle for an extended period of time, as it offers year round work covering a variety of produce.

The area produces both navel and valencia oranges, which are harvested at various times of the year. When there is a break from any of the citrus harvests, pruning work is available, so if you don't mind climbing a ladder, you could literally pick and prune all year round.

Like most regions in Australia, the grape harvest begins in February and finishes around late March, although in a late season, picking can continue through to April. Onions are also a big part of the overall crop in the area and harvesters are required during November and through until March.

Approximate numbers

About 7000 to 10,000 workers are required almost all year round.

Accommodation

Griffith Caravan Village. Tel: (02) 6962 3785.

Tourist Caravan Park. Tel: (02) 6964 2144.

Transport

Bus services operate from Melbourne and Sydney. A daily train service operates from Sydney. Your own transport would be helpful in getting to and from work.

Contacts

Miglnark Orchards, Griffith NSW 2680. Tel: (02) 6963 0034.

Miglnark Orchards specialises in growing citrus fruits. Orange picking is available between April and June and pay is piece rates by the bin. You can camp on site and facilities include a kitchen, fridge and showers.

Murray Mallee Training, Shop 3, 20 Banna Avenue, Griffith NSW 2680. Tel: (02) 6964 0400.

Tourist Information: 1800 681 141.

Citrus fruit growers

Bergamin O & M, Tharbogang NSW 2680. Tel: (02) 6963 6265.

Calabria M & B, 'The Oaks', Tharbogang NSW 2680. Tel: (02) 6963 6235.

Catania Farm, Farm 43, Hanwood NSW 2680. Tel: (02) 6963 0219.

Farm Fresh Direct, Lake Wyangan NSW 2680. Tel: (02) 6962 6025.

Ieraci S, 1818 Wyangan Avenue, Griffith NSW 2680. Tel: (02) 6962 3238.

McGann W, Farm 2399, Hanwood NSW 2680. Tel: (02) 6963 0142.

Parisotto P, Lake Wyangan NSW 2680. Tel: (02) 6962 3225.

Savage G, 'Ballingal', Tharbogang NSW 2680. Tel: (02) 6963 6217.

Scott F & A, Farm 1845, Lake Wyangan NSW 2680. Tel: (02) 6962 4894.

Vineyards

Baratto Wines, Griffith NSW 2680. Tel: (02) 6963 0171 or 0412 262 672.

De Bortoli Wines, De Bortoli Road, Bilbul NSW 2680. Tel: (02) 6964 9444.

McWilliams Wines, Hanwood NSW 2680. Tel: (02) 6963 0001.

Riverina Wines Farm, Farm 1810, Tharbogang NSW 2680. Tel: (02) 6963 6392.

Rossetto Wines, Rossetto Road, Beelbangera NSW 2680. Tel: (02) 6963 5214.

Terra Nova Estate, 60 Banna Avenue, Griffith NSW 2680. Tel: (02) 6962 1822.

The Cranswick Estate, Walla Avenue, Griffith NSW 2680. Tel: (02) 6962 4133.

Westend Wines, 1283 Brayne Road, Griffith NSW 2680. Tel: (02) 6964 1506.

Activities while you are there

Some of Australia's best known wineries are located in the area including De Bortoli and Hanwood, best known for its port. The Murrumbidgee River offers a host of water sports.

Hillston

North-west of Griffith is the small town of Hillston, which also offers a number of work options including oranges and potatoes.

Contacts

Hillston Citrus, Hillston NSW 2675. Tel: (02) 6967 2368.

Hillston Citrus offers seasonal pickers the opportunity to pick valencia oranges from September through to June.

Lampe Citrus, Hillston NSW 2675. Tel: (02) 6967 2540.

Lampe Citrus is a 500 acre orchard eight km from Hillston. Picking is from October to July and a typical days pay is $100 .

Rennie Produce, 'Moora Farm', River Road, Hillston NSW 2675. Tel: (02) 6967 4152.

Potatoes is what Rennie Produce are good at and there is plenty of harvest and processing work available between mid May to late September and mid November to mid January. For an eight hour day, you'll be paid around $100 (pre-tax) and the work is fairly demanding.

Leeton

Leeton is located in the heart of the Murrumbidgee Irrigation Area (MIA) and was the first town designed by the famous American architect, Walter Burley Griffin. It can also be called a government town, with many government departments located in the township.

Type of work

Leeton offers a variety of work options with a myriad of produce, including rice, stone fruits, oranges and grapes. The orange harvest kicks off in December and depending on the quality of the season, pickers can be required right through until May for valencia oranges and the winter months from June to August for navel oranges.

Leeton also has a developing grape industry and as with many other places around Australia, harvest time is February through until early April, with pruning during the cooler months.

Although not as large, the stone fruit industry does require pickers in February and March for mostly peaches and apricots.

Approximate numbers

The orange harvest requires more than 800 pickers while the grape harvest beginning in February requires 500 pickers. Stone fruits require 200 pickers. Remember that Leeton is still worth a visit in the cooler months for pruning work.

Accommodation

Gilgal Family Holiday Centre. Tel: (02) 6953 3882.

Leeton Caravan Park. Tel: (02) 6953 3323.

Leeton Hotel. Tel: (02) 6953 2027.

Transport

Daily bus and train connections to the town.

Contacts

Fruit Shack, Farm 312 Henry Lawson Drive, Leeton NSW 2705. Tel: 0429 866 965 or (02) 6953 2451.

The Fruit Shack is a fantastic place to both work and play. The focus is on travellers looking for work and accommodation. Picking and pruning work is available via the Fruit Shack, specifically in grapes and citrus fruits on nearby farms. On the play side of things, Mike from the Fruit Shack puts on some activities for travellers which include kangaroo spotting and a weekly disco in a double decker bus on the property. There is also an outdoor cinema for a restful evening after a hard days work. This property is definitely worth a look.

Murray Mallee Training Company, 9 Wade Avenue, Leeton NSW 2705. Tel: (02) 6953 7446.

Tourist Information. Tel: (02) 6953 2832.

Vegetable growers

Puntoriero's Produce, Farm 924, Whitton NSW 2705. Tel: (02) 6955 2616.

Citrus fruit growers

Auddino S & D, Farm 313, Wamoon NSW 2705. Tel: (02) 6955 9430.

Davidson P & J, Farm 838, Stanbridge NSW 2705. Tel: (02) 6955 1258.

Harrison J & K, Stanbridge NSW 2705. Tel: (02) 6955 1226.

Hillview Citrus, Robinson Road, Corbie Hill NSW 2705. Tel: (02) 6955 6205.

Morris J, Farm 326, Leeton NSW 2705. Tel: (02) 6955 9468.

Nardi N & C, Farm 337, Garner, Wamoon NSW 2705. Tel: (02) 6955 9565.

Williams I & M, Stanbridge NSW 2705. Tel: (02) 6955 1284.

Fruit and berry growers

Cedenco Australia, 'Wunamurra', Whitton NSW 2705. Tel: (02) 6955 2676.

Activities while you are there

At Easter every second year, Leeton holds a Country Festival. You can visit the Quelch juice factory, the Hydro Hotel built in 1919 and local wineries or go hot-air ballooning.

Moree

Moree is the local Aboriginal word for 'waterhole' and is 705 km north-west of Sydney and has a population of 10,460. The town is situated on the Mehi River and is home to one of Australia's largest cotton industries and Australia's first pecan nut farm, established in 1966.

Tourists flock to Moree for the famous spa baths, used by people suffering from arthritis or rheumatism and by workers from the cotton fields.

Type of work

Cotton chipping begins in late September and continues until February and requires many workers in and around the Moree region. The cotton harvest covers the months of April and May, and ginning (separating the cotton from its seeds) runs from April until July, and again many hands are required.

Approximate numbers

2000 workers are required during the various cotton processes.

Accommodation

Gwydir Caravan Park. Tel: (02) 6752 2723.

Mehi River Caravan Park. Tel: (02) 6752 7188.

Transport

A daily train service operates from Sydney and bus services operate from Brisbane and Melbourne.

Contacts

Best Employment, 26 Balo Street, Moree NSW 2400. Tel: (02) 6751 1444.

Joblink Plus, 135 Balo Street, Moree NSW 2400. Tel: 1800 627 564.

Gwydir Valley Cotton Growers Association, 207 Balo Street, Moree NSW 2400. Tel: (02) 6752 5652.

Cotton growers

Auscott, Mungindi Road, Moree NSW 2400. Tel: (02) 6759 1700.

Boree Cotton Loaders, 'Boree', Moree NSW 2400. Tel: (02) 6752 3163.

Brighann Ginning, 'Brighann', Watercourse Road, Moree NSW 2400. Tel: (02) 6753 3737.

Cotton Handling Systems, Moree NSW 2400. Tel: (02) 6752 5766.

Cotton Trading Corporation, PO Box 208, Moree NSW 2400. Tel: (02) 6752 7850.

Dunavant Enterprises, 21 Auburn Street, Moree NSW 2400. Tel: (02) 6759 1999.

Ecom Cotton Aust, 154 Heber Street, Moree NSW 2400. Tel: (02) 6752 4887.

Glen Cotton Co., 'The Glen', Ashley NSW 2400. Tel: (02) 6754 2165.

Lummus Australiad, 55 Tycannah Street, Moree NSW 2400. Tel: (02) 6751 1088.

Munro Module Movers, 'Boree', Boree Road, Moree NSW 2400. Tel: (02) 6752 5766.

Namoi Cotton Co-Operative, 191 Balo Street, Moree NSW 2400. Tel: (02) 6752 5339.

NM Rural Enterprises, Tellraga Station, Moree NSW 2400. Tel: (02) 6753 9537.

Queensland Cotton Corp, Max Centre, Moree NSW 2400. Tel: (02) 6752 5680.

Thornton & Co Cotton, Donor Cottage, Moree NSW 2400. Tel: (02) 6751 1010.

Turnbull, Roger, 'Wallam', Moree NSW 2400. Tel: (02) 6754 8615.

Volcot, 48 Auburn Street, Moree NSW 2400. Tel: (02) 6752 4822.

Activities while you are there

Check out the Moree Art Gallery which contains a great collection of authentic Aboriginal art. Other activities include fishing and swimming.

Mudgee

Around 300 km north west of Sydney, Mudgee is an increasingly popular short-visit destination for those from Sydney. They are attracted to the historical ambience of the town and nearby villages including Gulgong, the numerous wineries and the nature-based activities. With a population of about 8000, Mudgee relies on tourism and a range of agricultural and horticultural industries, a little different from the gold rush that spurred the growth of the town during the 1860s.

Type of work

With more than 150 wineries in the area it is the vineyards that require the greatest number of workers.

Approximate numbers

Several hundred are required for the picking during February and March and for pruning during the winter months.

Accommodation

There are a range of hotels, motels and caravan parks throughout the region.

Transport

There are regular coach services from Sydney along with trains.

Contacts

Willing Workers, 1800 782 385

Tourist Information. Tel: (02) 6372 1020.

Activities while you are there

Mudgee was settled in the 1820s, making it the second oldest town west of the Great Dividing Range, giving it and nearby villages including Gulgong, Hill End and Hargraves many historical buildings. The region's wineries are renown for the quality of their wine and there are many with cellar door sales. The natural areas including the nearby national parks provide space for bushwalking while Windamere Dam is a great place for swimming, boating or fishing.

Narrabri

Narrabri is 608 km north-west of Sydney and has a population of 7300. Known as the cotton capital of Australia, the Narrabri region is covered in white cotton between May and June, quite a sight for tourists!

Type of work

Like Moree, Narrabri offers the working traveller long periods of work in the cotton industry, covering chipping, harvest picking and ginning.

Approximate numbers

2000 workers are needed to cover the cotton process from chipping to ginning.

Accommodation

Council Caravan Park. Tel: (02) 6792 1294.

Transport

Own transport is required.

Contacts

Best Employment, 2 Bowen Street, Narrabri NSW 2390. Tel: 1800 660 662.

Cotton growers

Auscott Limited, Wee Waa Road, Narrabri NSW 2390. Tel: (02) 6799 1400.

Cotton Australia, PO Box 322, Narrabri NSW 2390. Tel: (02) 6792 6041.

Deltapine Australia, 60 Maitland Street, Narrabri NSW 2390. Tel: (02) 6792 5233.

Harpers Grain & Storage, Newell Highway, Narrabri NSW 2390. Tel: (02) 6792 4313.

NM Rural Enterprises, Togo Station, Narrabri NSW 2390. Tel: (02) 6795 7121.

Wire Lagoon, Wire Lagoon, Narrabri NSW 2390. Tel: (02) 6795 7162.

Activities while you are there

If you would like to try some rock climbing, check out Mount Kaputar National Park, located 53 km east of Narrabri. If rock climbing ain't your thing, there are short bushwalks in the area. Mount Kaputar is an extinct volcano and well worth the trip. You'll get a great view from the summit.

Narromine

Narromine has a population of 3390 and is located 444 km west of Sydney. Home of the Australian Gliding Championships, Narromine offers the working traveller much in the way of relaxation, as well as work in the region.

The town lies on the Macquarie River, which is the source of irrigation for the area, providing rich and fertile soil for growing a variety of crops including citrus fruits and cotton.

Type of work

Citrus orchards offer work from May right through to December, covering both navel and valencia harvests. The cotton work covers the months from December through to April/May, so if you are keen on staying around the area and can pick efficiently, Narromine maybe is a good place to settle down for a few months.

Approximate numbers

The citrus fruit industry requires at least 200 workers throughout the season. The cotton industry requires at least 1500 workers covering all facets of cotton processing.

Accommodation

Aerodrome Caravan Park. Tel: (02) 6889 2129.

The Old Farm Caravan Park. Tel: (02) 6889 1558.

Transport

Getting to Narromine is no problem via a train to Dubbo then a bus to Narromine. However, you will need to get around to seek work and once found, you'll need to drive to the farms, as accommodation is only available in town so your own vehicle is going to the easiest option.

Contacts

Narromine Community Skills, 6 Trangie Road, Narromine NSW 2821. Tel: (02) 6889 1422.

Tourist Information. Tel: (02) 6889 4596.

Cotton growers

A.F.M. Developments, 'Westwood', Narromine NSW 2821. Tel: (02) 6889 3334.

Australian Rural Commodities, 142 Terangion Street, Narromine NSW 2821. Tel: (02) 6889 4440.

Wirrigai Company, 'Wirrigai', Narromine NSW 2821. Tel: (02) 6889 2506.

Activities while you are there

Lazing on the banks of the Macquarie River will seem like heaven after a hard day's work. Otherwise head out to the aerodrome for some flying action.

Orange

Orange is situated 257 km west of Sydney and has a population of 33,000. Birthplace of the famous poet Banjo Paterson. Orange is a thriving, progressive rural centre that is surrounded by fertile land ideal for a large horticultural industry. Apart from its healthy horticultural industry, the Cadia Valley gold mine, situated 25 km from the township provides further employment for locals (water allowing).

Good restaurants, museums, Mount Canobolas adjacent to the township, and beautiful town gardens make Orange worth a visit, above and beyond seeking seasonal employment.

Type of work

The town of Orange is not known for oranges, but for apple orchards and a cherry industry! Harvest time for apples is March and April, while cherries are picked prior to Christmas in December. In addition to these traditional crops grown in the area, the viticulture industry has developed and further work opportunities exist during the grape harvest from February to early April.

Approximate numbers

The apple harvest requires at least 1500 pickers each season while 300 to 500 cherry pickers are required during the harvest.

Accommodation

Canobolas Caravan Park. Tel: (02) 6362 7279.

Transport

Daily train and bus services operate from Sydney.

Contacts

Orange Employment Service, 247 Anson Street, Orange NSW 2800. Tel: 02 6362 8169.

Tourist Information. Tel: (02) 6362 4215.

Apple and pear growers

Apple Factory, 14 Barretts Lane, Orange NSW 2800. Tel: (02) 6361 4431.

Carthew G, Pinnacle Road, Orange NSW 2800. Tel: (02) 6365 3231.

Claymont R & J, 'Winfield', Springside NSW 2800. Tel: (02) 6365 4261.

Cunial A & D, 'Carinya', Nashdale NSW 2800. Tel: (02) 6365 3172.

Darley P & J, 'Daydawn', Nashdale NSW 2800. Tel: (02) 6365 3278.

Emmi G & M, 30 Canobolas Road, Orange NSW 2800. Tel: (02) 6365 3326.

Gartrell D & C, 'Wattleview', Mt Lofty Road, Nashdale NSW 2800. Tel: (02) 6365 3233.

Kirkwood J, Stone Leigh Orchard, Orange NSW 2800. Tel: (02) 6365 8231.

New Apple Company of Orange, 14 Barrett Street, Orange NSW 2800. Tel: (02) 6361 9211.

Pearce R, 'Mirrabooka', Orange NSW 2800. Tel: (02) 6365 8216.

Perry K, 'Sunny Crest', Orange NSW 2800. Tel: (02) 6365 3239.

Rossetto Orchards, Ploughmans Lane, Orange NSW 2800. Tel: (02) 6361 4545.

Rossi Orchards, Mount Pleasant Lane, Orange NSW 2800. Tel: (02) 6365 3106.

Simpson, John Pastoral Co., Cargo Road, Orange NSW 2800. Tel: (02) 6361 4525.

Smith G, 'Walindi', Nashdale Lane, Nashdale NSW 2800. Tel: (02) 6365 3103.

Tree Top Fruit, RMB 24 Molong Road, Orange NSW 2800. Tel: (02) 6362 3935.

Treweek J, 'Thornbrook', Nashdale NSW 2800. Tel: (02) 6365 3215.

Vardanega D & J, 40 Pinnacle Road, Orange NSW 2800. Tel: (02) 6365 3242.

West E & J, Nashdale NSW 2800. Tel: (02) 6365 3102.

Williams B, 'The Pines', Lowenthal Lane, Nashdale NSW 2800. Tel: (02) 6365 3130.

Fruit and berry growers

Avondale Orchard Co, 37 Canobolas Road, Orange NSW 2800. Tel: (02) 6365 3414.

Borenore Berry Farm, 'Yalgogri', Borenore NSW 2800. Tel: (02) 6365 2296.

Cunich M, Nashdale NSW 2800. Tel: (02) 6365 3151.

Figtree Cottage & Orchard, Bradley Road, Borenore NSW 2800. Tel: (02) 6365 2225.

Floyd A, Phoenix Road, Lucknow NSW 2800. Tel: (02) 6365 5335.

Gale E, Uralla Shadforth NSW 2800. Tel: (02) 6368 7269.

Highland Heritage Farm, Bathurst Road, Orange NSW 2800. Tel: (02) 6361 3612.

Huntley Berry Farm, Huntley Road, via Orange NSW 2800. Tel: (02) 6365 5282.

Pascoe C, 37 Canobolas Road, Orange NSW 2800. Tel: (02) 6365 3414.

Activities while you are there

Mount Canobolas is worth a visit and if you pass through during the winter months you may find the peak covered in snow though it does not stay long. During the hot summer months, there's lots of bushwalking; and swimming in Lake Canobolas which offers relief from the heat. Orange also has some good restaurants to choose from for a splurge on decent food and wine.

Tumut

The township of Tumut sits in the Tumut Valley, and is one of the most beautiful places in Australia offering both an abundance of work and recreational options during your days off. Tumut is an Aboriginal word for 'resting place by the river', and one can do plenty of resting and exploring in the region.

Type of work

The apple harvest in the Tumut Valley region begins in February and can last through until late May. Cherries are picked over the months of December and January and the stone fruit harvest covers the period November to April.

Approximate numbers

The apple harvest requires at least 400 pickers while the cherry harvest is very season dependent and requirements can range from 30 in a poor season to 100 pickers in a good season. The stone fruit harvest requires around 300 pickers.

Accommodation

Blowering Holiday Park. Tel: (02) 6947 1383.

Riverglade Caravan Park. Tel: (02) 6947 2528.

Transport

You will need your own transport.

Contacts

Fruit and berry growers

Bella Vista Orchards, 4 Fords Lane, Tumut NSW 2720. Tel: (02) 6947 3263.

Heatley R, 'Bombowlee', Tumut NSW 2720. Tel: (02) 6947 2874.

Treetop Projects, 477 Wee Jasper Road, Tumut NSW 2720. Tel: (02) 6947 3788.

Wynyard Orchards, Batlow Road, Gilmore NSW 2720. Tel: (02) 6947 5276.

Activities while you are there

Tumut is perfectly located to make the most of the ski fields in the Kosciuszko National Park, which offers both downhill and cross-country skiing. Other activities include bushwalking, cave tours in the Yarrangobilly limestone caves, fishing and horse riding. If you're feeling a bit cold or have sore muscles from fruit picking, a thermal pool at the caves has a constant temperature of 27°C.

Wentworth

Located not far from Mildura but on the NSW side of the Murray River and at the point where it meets the Darling River Wentworth has a population of 1500. In its early days during the 1800s it was an important river port when paddle steamers made their way up and down the two rivers. Today it is a service town for the surrounding agricultural district and a tourist town.

Type of work

Wentworth is in the centre of the Sunraysia region known for its horticultural output. The region extends across the Murray River and includes the area around Mildura. The main crops are grapes, citrus and vegetables.

Approximate numbers

Depending on the time of year, several hundred workers are required.

Accommodation

There is a range of hotels, motels, caravan parks and hostels.

Transport

The Greyhound coach line passes though Mildura and the town is also serviced by the V Line from Melbourne. It's only a short way to Wentworth.

Contacts

Madec places seasonal job seekers throughout the Sunraysia region. In Wentworth telephone (03) 5027 2203. Web: www.madec.edu.au.

Tourist Information: Tel. (03) 5027 3624.

Activities while you are there

There are a number of historical attractions in the town but the rivers provide some respite from work, more so during the hotter parts of the year when much of the work is undertaken. Further a field there is the Mungo National Park with its bleak moonscape like features and Scotia Sanctuary.

Young

Young is a very popular spot for working travellers, and is known for its cherry and stone fruit industries. Located 378 km south-west of Sydney and with a population of 6600, Young presents many work opportunities, although limited to only a few months of the year.

Type of work

A massive influx of workers sets up camp in late October/early November in time for the cherry harvest, which occurs over the months of November and December and reaps the equivalent of over 70 per cent of Australia's cherry crop.

After a quieter month in January, the work prospects pick up again with the prune harvest covering the months of February and March.

Approximate numbers

The cherry harvest requires up to 4000 pickers with additional work in packing and grading the produce. The prune harvest requires numbers in the vicinity of 500 to 600 workers over February and March.

Accommodation

Young Tourist Park. Tel: (02) 6382 2190.

Transport

Daily train and bus connections operate from Sydney.

Contacts

Bats Fruit, 'Cherrymore', Wombat Road, Young NSW 2594. Tel: (02) 6384 3222.

Bats Fruit orchard grows cherry and stone fruits and pickers are required from late November until Christmas for cherries and from early February to March for stone fruits. Pay is by piece rates, varying from $100 to $180 per day (pre-tax) for a six to eight hour day.

Cherry Haven Orchards, Cowra Road, Young NSW 2594. Tel: (02) 6382 4023.

Cherry Haven Orchards is a cherry and plum orchard which requires pickers in early November for six to eight weeks. A normal day starts at 6.30 a.m. and ends at 2.30 p.m. and you are paid on the amount of fruit picked.

Fairview Orchard, Cowra Road, Young NSW 2594. Tel: (02) 6382 1686.

Fairview Orchard grows cherries and stone fruit. Pickers are required from early November to mid December and also from late January through to March for eight weeks. Pay is by the amount of fruit you pick and an average picker's wage is $400 per week (pre-tax).

Young Employment Service, 76 Main Street, Young NSW 2594. Tel: (02) 6382 5098.

Young Tourist Information. Tel: (02) 6382 5085.

Fruit and berry growers

Abbas & Sons Cherry Orchard, Wombat Road, Young NSW 2594. Tel: (02) 6382 7030.

Arabin A & B, Virginia Orchard, Young NSW 2594. Tel: (02) 6382 5091.

Bunavale Orchards, Jasprizza Lane, Young NSW 2594. Tel: (02) 6382 3931.

Cherry Growers Co-Op, Cowra Road, Young NSW 2594. Tel: (02) 6382 2513.

Cherryhaven Orchards, 'Cherryhaven', Cowra Road, Young NSW 2594. Tel: (02) 6382 4023.

Cunich E & Co, Cowra Road, Young NSW 2594. Tel: (02) 6382 5995.

Equitas Orchards, Back Creek Road, Young NSW 2594. Tel: (02) 6382 1479.

Harvey M, Wickham Lane, Young NSW 2594. Tel: (02) 6382 3071.

Jasprizza R & P, Cowra Road, Young NSW 2594. Tel: (02) 6382 2513.

Levett P, 'Heatherlea', Maimura, NSW 2594. Tel: (02) 6383 3276.

Lynton Orchards, Olympic Way, Young NSW 2594. Tel: (02) 6382 1685.

O'Brien T & S, Cowra Road, Young NSW 2594. Tel: (02) 6382 2384.

Sugarsun Farm, Spring Creek, Young NSW 2594. Tel: (02) 6382 2252.

Thompson G, Wombat Road, Young NSW 2594. Tel: (02) 6384 3249.

Activities while you are there

Activities include visits to wineries and bushwalking. In town be sure to check out the Lambing Flat Folk Museum and Burrangong Art Gallery.

Harvest trail - Victoria

Cobram

Cobram lies on the Murray River, 252 km north of Melbourne, with a population of 4600. The area has abundant fruit growing and is also a popular holiday destination. On the banks of the Murray River close to the township and near the bridge, you'll find Thompson's Beach for swimming, water skiing and picnics.

Type of work

Your first stop for work is the Victorian Peach and Apricot Growers Association, which represents over 100 growers in the area during the harvest season from December to April. During the peak harvest season, they are open from 10 a.m. to 1 p.m. Monday to Friday.

Approximate numbers

Over 2500 pickers are needed during the harvest season.

Accommodation

Cobram Classic Motel. Tel: (03) 5872 1633.

A number of growers have accommodation on site.

Transport

Cobram can be reached easily by train and bus.

Contacts

Victorian Peach and Apricot Growers Association, 30A Bank Street, Cobram VIC 3644. Tel: (03) 5872 1729. Fax: (03) 5871 1612.

Tourist Information. Tel: (03) 5872 2132.

Apple and pear growers

Morgante B, Cobram South Road, Cobram VIC 3644. Tel: (03) 5872 1369.

Orchards J, Lot 1 Campbells Road, Cobram VIC 3644. Tel: (03) 5871 1485.

Peach-A-Rosa D'Amore, Murray Valley Highway, Cobram VIC 3644. Tel: (03) 5871 2710.

Pullar P , Murray Valley Highway, Cobram VIC 3644. Tel: (03) 5872 2222.

Fruit and berry growers

Boosey Fruit, Chapel Road, Cobram VIC 3644. Tel: (03) 5873 5390.

Capri Orchard, O'Brien Road, Yarroweyah VIC 3644. Tel: (03) 5873 2360.

Diaco G, Cottons Road, Cobram VIC 3644. Tel: (03) 5871 1568.

Gattuso G, Cobram VIC 3644. Tel: (03) 5872 1170.

KNM Strawberries, Kangan Road, Koonoomoo VIC 3644. Tel: (03) 5871 1992.

MacHeda D, Healy Road, Yarroweyah VIC 3644. Tel: (03) 5872 2375.

Mete P & L, Lonergan Road, Cobram VIC 3644. Tel: (03) 5873 2384.

Nicosia J & N, Catona Crescent, Cobram VIC 3644. Tel: (03) 5872 1683.

Orsida M & L, Murray Valley Highway, Cobram VIC 3644. Tel: (03) 5872 1252.

Raco J, 14 Wondah Street, Cobram VIC 3644. Tel: (03) 5872 1821.

Scenic Drive Strawberries, Torgannah Road, Koonoomoo VIC 3644. Tel: (03) 5871 1263.

Sonnet Orchards, Karook Street, Cobram VIC 3644. Tel: (03) 5872 1679.

Treestone Orchards, Cottons Road, Cobram VIC 3644. Tel: (03) 5871 1267.

Activities while you are there

Activities include water sports, touring the area, visiting wineries and the Cobram Matata Deer farm.

Echuca

Echuca is an Aboriginal word for 'meeting of the waters' and this couldn't be more apt for the geographical position of this friendly and historical township located 220 km north of Melbourne. Echuca is situated at the meeting point of the Murray, Campaspe and Goulburn rivers and is one of the oldest river towns in Victoria.

From a tourist point of view, Echuca has many sites to discover, including the Echuca Historical Society Museum, World in Wax Museum and the Coach House Carriage Collection. Alternatively, if you wanted a lazy few days floating up and down the river, you can hire a houseboat in Echuca.

Type of work

Tomatoes are the main crop in the Echuca area, although with the explosive growth of the Australian wine industry, landowners in and around Echuca are catching on to the demand for wine. However, at the time of writing, yields are still very low due to the young age of the vines. Tomato harvest takes place from February to March however, work is available in maintaining the plants prior to harvest.

Approximate numbers

Over 600 workers are required, depending on the season.

Accommodation

Echuca Gardens B&B and Hostel, 103 Mitchell Street, Echuca VIC 3564. Tel: (03) 5480 6522.

There are plenty of caravan parks in the area.

Transport

Daily bus service connecting to Melbourne, Canberra and Sydney.

Contacts

Tourist Information. Tel: (03) 5480 7555.

Vineyards

Port Of Call Wine Centre, Radcliffe Street, Echuca VIC 3564. Tel: (03) 5480 2005.

Tisdall Wines, 19 Cornelia Creek Road, Echuca VIC 3564. Tel: (03) 5482 1911.

Activities while you are there

The rivers offer a number of water-based activities including swimming, fishing and houseboat cruising. The town also has a number of annual festivals including the Rich River Festival in October and the Southern 80 water ski race in February.

Mildura

Mildura is located 550 km north-west of Melbourne and has a population of 17,990. Sitting on the banks of the Murray River, Mildura is home to a large citrus and viticulture industry, which attracts thousands of people every harvest. In fact, over the last few years, the area has made the news in major cities stating its urgent need for more workers to join in the harvest season.

Mildura is Aboriginal for 'red earth', which is a fitting description given the region's darkish red soil. In the 1880s an irrigation system was set up to feed the land from the Murray River, and thus began the citrus industry. Today, farmers are also using the land for other produce including grapes and olives. Apart from making wine, some of the region's grapes are also used as sultanas and table grapes.

In the township of Mildura you will find a fantastic Information Centre and Citrus Shop, where you can learn much about the citrus industry in what is known as the Sunraysia District. Mildura is a very popular tourist destination, with plenty to see and do, above and beyond fruit picking.

Type of work

The area offers fantastic opportunities for work. In fact, there is something to pick no matter what time of year you are there. Both navel and valencia oranges are grown by over 700 growers in the region. Harvest takes place throughout the year, depending on the type of orange grown. Additional work can be sought in the off-season in pruning and other orchard maintenance.

The grape harvest begins in February and concludes in early April, and from a work point of view, opens many opportunities with thousands of workers required to take the fruit from the vines.

Your first point of contact should be with Madec Jobs Australia, who have the task of operating the Mildura Harvest Labour Office. See their website: www.madec.edu.au.

Approximate numbers

Over 1500 workers are required for the orange harvest and 1200 to 1500 for the grape harvest.

Accommodation

Rosemont Guest House, 154 Madden Avenue, Mildura VIC 3500. Tel: (03) 5023 1535.

There are plenty of caravan parks and youth hostels in the area.

Transport

Daily bus and train services from Melbourne to Adelaide and Sydney.

Contacts

Altus Personnel, 105 Orange Avenue, Mildura VIC 3500. Tel: (03) 5023 8840.

Madec Jobs Australia, Cnr Tenth St & Deakin Ave, Mildura VIC 3500. Tel: (03) 5022 1797.

Mildura Fruit Company, The Crescent, Mildura VIC 3500. Tel: (03) 5021 1644.

Zippy Koala, 206 Eighth St, Mildura VIC 3500. Tel: (03) 5021 5793.

Citrus fruit growers

Lloyd R & D, Paringi VIC 3500. Tel: (03) 5024 0224.

Sunraysia Citrus Growers, 58 Pine Avenue, Mildura VIC 3500. Tel: (03) 5023 8205.

Vineyards

Carn Estate Wines, 453 Deakin Avenue, Mildura VIC 3500. Tel: (03) 5021 1011.

Macri J & L, Block 411, Mourquong, Mildura VIC 3500. Tel: (03) 5022 2931.

Rosemount Estate, 27 Jubilee Drive, Mildura VIC 3500. Tel: (03) 5023 8671.

Tall Poppy Wines, 82 Lemon Avenue, Mildura VIC 3500. Tel: (03) 5027 4000.

Activities while you are there

Activities include water sports, visiting wineries and Mungo National Park and horse riding. There are also a number of festivals that take place throughout the year including the Sunraysia Wine and Jazz Festival during November, Country Music Week in September and the Festival of the Oasis Rose during November. A number of paddleboats provide river cruises from Mildura but only one is still a genuine paddle-steamer and that is PS Melbourne which runs a daily two-hour cruise.

Robinvale

Robinvale is a small town on the Victorian side of the Murray River with a population of approximately 2000. It's the ideal spot to both relax and get some work during the harvest times for a variety of produce grown in the area.

Robinvale lies between Mildura and Swan Hill along the Murray River, and although much smaller in population, the region can offer many months of work for the working traveller.

Type of work

Originally known for its grape crop, Robinvale has diversified and now offers job opportunities in vegetables and citrus fruits. Having stated that, the majority of work to be found in the area focuses on the grape harvest, beginning in early February and running through until April. During the off-season, from September to October, there is also work in thinning the vines, although the numbers required for this task are substantially fewer than those required at harvest time.

Vegetables are picked and packed at various times during the year, as are citrus fruits, although the numbers required are fewer than for the grape harvest.

Approximate numbers

Up to 4000 workers are needed during the grape harvest, 500

for the off-season pruning of grape vines and 300 to 600 for vegetable picking.

Accommodation

Riverside Caravan Park. Tel: (03) 5026 4646.

Weir Caravan Park. Tel: (03) 5026 3415.

Transport

Bus and train services operate daily to Mildura from where you can grab a ride to Robinvale.

Contacts

Boyanda Happy Valley, Robinvale VIC 3549. Tel: (03) 5026 9285.

Madec Jobs Australia, Robinvale Resource Centre, 68-72 Herbert Street, Robinvale VIC 3549. Tel: (03) 5023 4300.

Murray Mallee Training Group, Hobart Street, Robinvale VIC 3549. Tel: 0409 003 371.

Citrus fruits growers

Murray G & D, Tol Tol VIC 3549. Tel: (03) 5026 3847.

Payne P & C, Tol Tol Road, Robinvale VIC 3549. Tel: (03) 5026 3867.

Vegetable growers

Happy Valley Enterprises, Hocking Road, Bannerton VIC 3549. Tel: (03) 5026 9366.

Olivegrove Trading Company, Tol Tol Road, Robinvale VIC 3549. Tel: (03) 5026 3814.

Vineyards

Manna V & J, Hocking Road, Robinvale VIC 3549. Tel: (03) 5026 3986.

Robinvale Organic Wines, Sealake Road, Robinvale VIC 3549. Tel: (03) 5026 3955.

Sylvester A & K, Hattah Bannerton Road, Wemen VIC 3549. Tel: (03) 5026 0250.

Activities while you are there

Swimming and relaxing on the Murray River.

Rochester

Rochester is approximately 50 km south of Echuca and 180 km north of Melbourne. The region is known for its tomatoes, although more recently grape vines and olives have made their way into the paddocks.

Rochester was originally known as Rowe's Camp, then Rowechester and finally, in 1865 was named Rochester. It's an area irrigated by nearby reservoirs, such as the Waranga Basin and Lake Eppalock, and apart from tomatoes, grapes and olives, is also home to a substantial dairy industry.

Type of work

Due to the young grape and olive industries, planting and weeding are the main tasks available throughout the year, although the numbers required are small.

Much of the tomato work is done mechanically, however tractor drivers, sorters and packers are required during the harvest period from February to May.

Your first point of contact should be JBEK Employment. They offer a variety of work in the district including picking, pruning and tractor and forklift driving.

Approximate numbers

Up to 1000 workers are required for the tomato harvest, and 200 on the grape and olive farms.

Accommodation

Rochester Motel. Tel: (03) 5484 1077.

Transport

Train and bus services from Melbourne.

Contacts

JBEK Employment, 41 Mackay Street, Rochester VIC 3561. Tel: (03) 5484 3696.

Activities while you are there

Activities include fishing, golf, horse riding and water sports and having a vehicle makes these activities more accessible.

Shepparton

Shepparton is situated 182 km north of Melbourne and has a population of 25,450. The area around Shepparton has rich fertile land watered by the Goulburn River irrigation system. Since the development of the irrigation system in 1912, the district has developed into a very large agricultural and horticultural area, which includes orchards, vegetables, dairying and beef cattle.

The Shepparton Preserving Company (SPC) is one of Australia's oldest canneries. The factory is open to the public and products can be purchased directly from the factory. Other food processing factories include Campbell's Soups, Kraft Foods and Ardmona Foods. To relax around Shepparton many locals and tourists venture to Victoria Park. It has a 20 ha lake which provides a home to local wildlife.

Type of work

The majority of picking work revolves around the fruit harvest, which starts just before Christmas and peaks in late January to early February. Fruits produced in the area include pears, apricots, apples and peaches, while tomatoes make up the main vegetable crop, which is harvested in January through until late March.

Due to the number of canneries and processing factories in the area, further work can be obtained throughout the year by applying for work directly with these companies.

Approximate numbers

In excess of 10,000 workers are required during the harvest season.

Accommodation

There are many caravan parks throughout the township, and you may also find it worthwhile asking employers if accommodation is available on-site.

Transport

Shepparton is a very central location in Victoria, making it easy to reach from Melbourne.

Contacts

Tourist Information. Tel: (03) 5831 4400.

Fruit growers

Ahmet Brothers, Shepparton East VIC 3631. Tel: (03) 5829 2252.

Arden Orchards, Paul Road, Lemnos VIC 3631. Tel: (03) 5829 9345.

Australian Horticultural Corporation, 140 Welsford Street, Shepparton VIC 3630. Tel: (03) 5831 3919.

Damchev Orchard, 625 Midland Highway, Shepparton East VIC 3631. Tel: (03) 5829 2241.

Fairless Orchards, Hanlon Road, Shepparton East VIC 3631. Tel: (03) 5829 2210.

Guppy N & K, 445 Channel Road, Shepparton East VIC 3631. Tel: (03) 5829 2214.

Pottenger J & J, 645 Central Avenue, Shepparton East VIC 3631. Tel: (03) 5829 2371.

Prentice J & B, Prentice Road, Orrvale VIC 3631. Tel: (03) 5829 2606.

Sali W, Verney Road, Shepparton VIC 3630. Tel: 0417 506 200.

Silverstein M & C, 131 Prentice Road, Shepparton East VIC 3631. Tel: (03) 5829 2307.

Sofra P, Benalla Road, Shepparton VIC 3630. Tel: (03) 5821 3568.

Suncity Orchards, Hosies Road, Shepparton East VIC 3631. Tel: (03) 5829 1065.

Tirana Coolstores, 180 Channel Road, Orrvale VIC 3631. Tel: (03) 5821 5241.

Tyers M & G, Shepparton East VIC 3631. Tel: (03) 5829 2336.

Ymer J, Prentice Road, Orrvale VIC 3631. Tel: (03) 5829 2561.

Activities while you are there

Activities include fishing, water sports, scenic drives around the area visiting the many smaller towns in the district.

Swan Hill

Swan Hill is located 343 km north-west of Melbourne and has a population of 9600. It is a large regional town on the banks of the

Murray River that offers plenty of work all year round. The town was first settled in 1840 by explorer Thomas Mitchell and was aptly named after the black swans in the area.

For both locals on holidays and tourists, Swan Hill offers the perfect place to relax and enjoy the serenity of the mighty Murray River, while south of the town is Lake Boga, used for a number of recreational pursuits including fishing, water skiing and parasailing.

Type of work

The region's main produce is grapes and stone fruits, while there is also a smaller vegetable industry that requires pickers in the early part of the year.

The grape harvest begins in February and finishes around April, although in a good season this can extend until May. The stone fruit industry is very large, and workers can expect to begin the harvest as early as November and work through until late March to early April. Work in the packing sheds is also available late in the harvest season.

During the winter months work can be found pruning vines and orchard trees.

Approximate numbers

The grape harvest requires more than 2000 workers. The stone fruit harvest requires more than 1000 workers, and work is also available in pruning during the cooler months.

Accommodation

There are a number of caravan parks in the area to cater for large numbers of tourists.

Transport

Train and connecting bus services run from Melbourne.

Contacts

Bulga Wine Estates, Bulga Road, Swan Hill VIC 3585. Tel: (03) 5037 6685.

Madec Jobs, 186-188 Beveridge Street, Swan Hill VIC 3585. Tel: (03) 5033 0025.

Murray Mallee Training (Swan Hill), 335-339 Campbell Street, Swan Hill VIC 3585. Tel: (03) 5033 1216.

Swan Hill Vineyards, Woorinen Road, Swan Hill VIC 3585. Tel: (03) 5037 6972.

Activities while you are there

Check out the paddle steamers on the river, water sports, fishing, horse riding and the Burke and Wills Tree on Curlewis Street, which was planted over 100 years ago to commemorate the arrival of these explorers in the area. The tree is believed to be the largest of its kind in Australia.

Yarra Valley

Only about 50 km east of Melbourne, the Yarra Valley and the Dandenongs are both close to a major city yet distant in terms of rural tranquil. There are numerous small towns scattered throughout this region and about 30 wineries in the valley produce some of the best cool-climate wines in the country.

Type of work

The seasonal work focuses on the vineyards but there are also other crops such as apples, cherries and pears.

Approximate numbers

Several hundred for picking grapes, apples and cherries.

Accommodation

Hotels, motels, caravan parks and hostels are scattered throughout the region.

Transport

Trains arrive frequently from Melbourne in the Dandenongs and local buses are available but having your own car is the ideal option.

Contacts

Sarina Russo Job Access has an office in Lilydale which can advise on seasonal employment in the valley. Tel: (03) 9735 7800. Web: http://sarinarusso.com.au.

Activities while you are there

There are many historical sites in the region along with outdoor activities aplenty. Puffing Billy, the steam train takes you on a 25 km journey through the forest, but if you prefer walking there are endless trails in the nearby national parks and state forests.

Harvest trail - Tasmania

Gunns Plains

The Gunns Plains region is located close to the north coast of Tasmania. Close by are the cities of Burnie and Devonport, while the major town in the area is Ulverstone, 300 km north-west of Hobart.

Ulverstone is a seaside resort with a population of 9900, which, as one of Tasmania's tourist towns, swells during holiday periods.

Type of work

The Gunns Plains area offers diversity in produce. Flower picking over the months of December and January requires experienced pickers, but the numbers aren't great so ensure you enlist early. At the same time raspberries and strawberries come into season and there are a number of raspberry and strawberry farms to choose from. As with flower picking, be early to get work because pickers are only required in small numbers.

Cherries come into season in December and workers are needed before Christmas. Vegetables including capsicums, beans, zucchinis, squash and pumpkin come into season from January through to March and are probably your safest bet for work.

Other work in the region includes harvesting hops but this normally requires those experienced in driving farm machinery. Onions are also grown in the area and you may land a job picking or sorting these in the packing sheds.

Approximate numbers

Raspberry and strawberry crops in the region require anywhere between 80 and 160 pickers, although the fruit is very sensitive to seasonal variation and therefore numbers can vary greatly from year to year. The vegetables harvest requires 100 to 300 workers between

January and March while the flower harvest requires only a small numbers of workers with preference given to workers with experience in flower picking.

Accommodation

MacWright House YHA Hostel, 115 Middle Road, Devonport TAS 7310. Tel: (03) 6424 5696.

Tasman House, 114 Tasman Street, Devonport TAS 7310. Tel: (03) 6423 2335.

The Lighthouse Hotel. Tel: (03) 6425 1197.

Transport

Bus service from Burnie, Devonport and Launceston.

Contacts

Forth Farm, Leith Road, Forth TAS 7310. Tel: (03) 6428 2505.

Botanical Resources, 115 Eastland Drive, Ulverstone TAS 7315. Tel: (03) 6425 5888.

Tourist information. Tel: (03) 6425 2839.

Vegetable growers

Brandsema J & A, 8 Brandsema Street, Turners Beach TAS 7315. Tel: (03) 6428 2319.

Rodman, R & D, 969 Castra Road, Sprent TAS 7315. Tel: (03) 6429 3181.

Activities while you are there

Fishing, golf and water sports. You can also saddle up for the Twilight Rodeo in February or check out the Agricultural Show in October.

Huon Valley

The Huon Valley is the centre of apple growing in Tasmania. The key town in the area is Huonville, which is situated 42 km south-west of Hobart and has a modest population of 1520 people.

Huonville is located on the Huon River, which is a popular destination for thrill-seekers jumping on high speed motor boats for a heart stopping ride down the river. The area is also known for its freshwater fishing, in particular large rainbow trout.

Other towns worth a visit in the area include Geeveston and Cygnet. Geeveston is best known as an entry point to the rugged Hartz Mountains National Park, which is frequented by cross-country skiers in winter and adventurous bushwalkers during the warmer months.

Type of work

As mentioned earlier, apples are the main source of work in this region. At harvest time, thousands of workers are required to pick the fruit in the orchards. Picking time is between March and April, while there is still plenty of maintenance work including thinning and pruning and other general tasks prior to Christmas. Pears are also grown in the area and follow a similar harvest pattern to apples.

Cherries and strawberries are also grown in the valley, and although the yield compared to the enormous apple industry remains small, occasional work may be available.

Approximate numbers

Up to 3000 workers are required over the apple harvest, while 100 to 200 are required for the cherry and strawberry harvests.

Accommodation

Adelphi Court YHA Hostel, 17 Stoke Street, New Town TAS 7008. Tel: (03) 6228 4829.

Budget Bunks (Ocean Child Hotel), 86 Argyle Street, Hobart TAS 7000. Tel: (03) 6234 6730.

Central City Backpackers, 138 Collins Street, Hobart TAS 7000. Tel: (03) 6224 2404.

Transport

There is a daily bus service from Hobart, although your own transport is advisable.

Contacts

Tourist Information. Tel: (03) 6297 1836.

Apple and pear growers

Bond B & E, 'Brookside', 49 Lonnavale Road, Judbury TAS 7109.

Tel: (03) 6266 0251.

Calvert Bros, Waterloo TAS 7109. Tel: (03) 6297 6264.

Clark R, Glen Road, Huonville TAS 7109. Tel: (03) 6264 1034.

Duggan L & S, 8464 Channel Highway, Cradoc TAS 7109. Tel: (03) 6266 3319.

Griggs Grower Direct, 873 Huon Highway, Huonville TAS 7109. Tel: (03) 6264 1474.

Hansen Orchards, Grove TAS 7109. Tel: (03) 6266 4065.

Heron R, Cool Store Road, Huonville TAS 7109. Tel: (03) 6264 1024.

Salter A, North Huon Road, Huonville TAS 7109. Tel: (03) 6264 1446.

Scott Bros, Cairns Bay TAS 7109. Tel: (03) 6297 1230.

Smith, I & D, 54 Lucaston Road, Grove TAS 7109. Tel: (03) 6266 4587.

Townsend A & G, 8736 Channel Highway, Woodstock TAS 7109. Tel: (03) 6266 3213.

Fruit and berry growers

Hansen Orchards, Grove TAS 7109. Tel: (03) 6266 4236.

Kile Horticultural, Thompsons Road, Grove TAS 7109. Tel: (03) 6264 1159.

Tassie Blue Blueberries, Cygnet Coast Road, Lymington TAS 7109. Tel: (03) 6295 1795.

Tru-Blu Berries, 78 Cygnet Coast Road, Lymington TAS 7109. Tel: (03) 6295 0082.

Activities while you are there

Sunday markets are held on the river bank, as well as the Festival on the Bank, which is held in April. During your stay, activities include fishing for big trout in the rivers, jet boat rides and other water sports.

Tamar Valley

The Tamar Valley is located just north of Launceston and therefore offers the working traveller the best of both worlds: a beautiful place to work and the opportunity to relax and have fun in a city with a population of some 68,700, which is second only in size to Hobart which has a population of 128,600. Bushwalking and skiing at nearby Ben Lomand National Park is an option.

Type of work

The Tamar Valley region, long known for its apples, requires workers for the harvest between late February and May each year. However, over recent years, grape production has been on the increase and Tasmania is becoming known for its cool climate varieties including the well known pinot noir. Today, many new vineyards are planting for the future and this opens opportunities for work in the region, even during non-harvest times, as the young vines need care and nurturing. In respect to mature vines, harvest time is February to April.

Approximate numbers

The grape harvest requires between 800 and 1000 pickers during February and April while the apple harvest requires approximately 1000 workers over the harvest period.

Accommodation

Batman Inn, 35-39 Cameron Street, Launceston TAS 7250. Tel: (03) 6331 7222.

Launceston City Backpackers, 173 George Street, Launceston TAS 7250. Tel: (03) 6334 2327.

Launceston City Youth Hostel, 36 Thistle Street, Launceston TAS 7250. Tel: (03) 6344 9779.

Riverview, 43 Charles Street, Launceston TAS 7250. Tel: (03) 633 4857.

Transport

Although there are local bus services in and around the Tamar Valley, you'll need your own transport to reach the many orchards and vineyards in the region.

Contacts

Tamar Visitor Information Centre. Tel: (03) 6394 4454.

Tourist Information for the Launceston area. Tel: (03) 6336 3122.

Apple and pear growers

Lees Orchards, Dilston TAS 7252. Tel: (03) 6328 1229.

Millar L & Co., 'Rewa', 124 Craigburn Road, Hillwood TAS 7252. Tel: (03) 6394 8191.

Miller G & Sons, Main Road, Hillwood TAS 7252. Tel: (03) 6394 8181.

Sweetwater Pears, 411 Los Angelos Road, Swan Bay TAS 7252. Tel: (03) 6328 1309.

Activities while you are there

The sheep and wool industry in Tasmania has played an important part in the state's economy. The Tamar Knitting Mill, which is Tasmania's largest mill, is a great place to check out with daily tours through the mill. In Launceston, there are many festivals throughout the year including Festivals in February, which incorporates food, wine, entertainment and the arts, while the Royal Launceston Show takes place in October.

Harvest trail - South Australia

Adelaide Hills

The city of Adelaide is surrounded to the south and east by rolling hills, known as the Mount Lofty Ranges, which are home to many fruit orchards. Being in very close proximity to the city of Adelaide, the hills offer the best of both worlds, with the ability to work in the orchards during the week, while relaxing on weekends in Australia's fifth largest city with a population of a bit over one million people.

Type of work

Your first stop in seeking employment in the region should be in the small township of Lenswood, where you'll find a growers co-operative which should point you in the right direction for both picking and packing shed work. During harvest season from February to late April, gate calling and dropping into the many youth hostels in Adelaide should also assist you in landing picking and packing work.

The outer reaches of Adelaide also offer grape picking and pruning, and again talking to locals, looking on job boards in hostels and contacting employment agencies in the region will assist you in locating work during harvest season and during pruning season in the cooler winter months.

Approximate numbers

During harvest season for apples and pears, the region can expect to employ up to 800 casual pickers and packers. The grape harvest in the area can also provide work for in excess of 500 pickers.

Accommodation

With the Adelaide Hills less than one hours drive from the city, accommodation can be found in the city and in numerous caravan parks scattered throughout Adelaide and nearby areas.

New World International Backpackers, 29 Crompton Street, Adelaide SA 5000. Tel: (08) 821 26 888.

Backpack Oz, 144 Wakefield Street, Adelaide SA 5000. Tel: (08) 8223 3551.

Sunny's Backpackers, 139 Franklin Street, Adelaide SA 5000. Tel: (08) 8231 2430.

Rucksackers Riders, 257 Gillies Street, Adelaide SA 5000. Tel: (08) 823 2 0823.

Nomads Cumberland Arms Hotel, 205 Waymouth Street, Adelaide SA 5000. Tel: (08) 8231 357.

Adelaide YHA, 290 Gillies Street, Adelaide SA 5000. Tel: (08) 8223 6007.

Adelaide City Backpackers Hostel, 237-239 Franklin Street, Adelaide SA 5000. Tel: (08) 8212 2668.

Adelaide Backpackers Inn, 112 Carrington Street, Adelaide SA 5000. Tel: (08) 8223 6635.

Transport

A daily bus service travels from Adelaide city to the major Adelaide Hills townships. Call the Passenger Transport Board on (08) 8210 1000 for more information.

Contacts

Drake International, Level 7, 111 Gawler Place, Adelaide SA 5000. Tel (08) 9321 9911.

Employment Options, 3/221 Dutton Road, Mt Barker SA 5251. Tel (08) 8398 2355.

Torrens Valley Orchards, Forreston Road, Gumeracha SA 5233. (08) 83891405.

Tourist Information. Tel: 1800 353 323 (Hahndorf) or (08) 830 1054 (Mount Lofty).

Apple and pear growers

MacDonald Fruit, Powell Road, Kersbrook SA 5231. Tel: (08) 8389 3203.

Newman's Produce, Newman Road, Cudlee Creek SA 5232. Tel: (08) 8389 2267.

Plummers Border Valley Orchards, Jackson Hill Road, Gumeracha SA 5233. Tel: (08) 8389 1124.

Ross KR & LN, Kersbrook SA 5231. Tel: (08) 8389 3094.

Grape growers

Angas Creek Vineyard, Angas Creek Road, Gumeracha SA 5233. Tel: (08) 8568 5625.

Chain Of Ponds Wines, Main Road, Gumeracha SA 5233. Tel: (08) 8389 1415.

Gumeracha Vineyards, Main Road, Gumeracha SA 5233. Tel: (08) 8389 1459.

Talunga Wines and Restaurant, Adelaide, Mannum Road, Gumeracha SA 5233. Tel: (08) 8389 1222.

Strawberry growers

Netherhill Strawberry Farm, Netherhill Road, Kenton Valley SA 5233. Tel: (08) 8389 1046.

Activities while you are there

Spend your spare time both in Adelaide city and the townships in and around the hills. Adelaide is also a city of festivals, including the Fringe Festival in February, the Royal Adelaide Show in late August and early September and the International Rose Show in October.

Barossa Valley

The Barossa Valley is just 40 km from Adelaide and is one of Australia's premier wine districts. Many towns make up the region including Gawler with a population of 11,500, Nuriootpa with 3350 and Angaston with 2000. The area has a strong German heritage, and every year thousands of tourists, both domestic and international, visit the Barossa to tour the many wineries in the district.

The wine industry in the Barossa is high yielding, with over 45,000 tonnes of grapes picked both mechanically and by hand every season.

Type of work

There is certainly a wealth of opportunity for the working traveller, during both harvest time from February to April and pruning during the winter months. In addition to pickers and pruners, the area also caters to a large tourist industry and therefore hospitality work is also available, particularly during the busy times of the year. The best method of finding work is to call directly on restaurants, cafes and bars.

Approximate numbers

The grape harvest requires 400 to 600 pickers and over 400 pruners are needed during the winter months.

Accommodation

Barossa Valley Caravan Park. Tel: (08) 8562 1404.

Gawler Caravan Park. Tel: (08) 8522 3805.

Transport

Daily bus service from Adelaide.

Contacts

Employment Directions, 54 Main Road, Clare SA 5453. Tel: (08) 8842 2945.

Tourist Information. Tel: (08) 8562 2627.

Grape growers

Elderton Wines, 3 Tanunda Road, Nuriootpa SA 5355. Tel: (08) 8562 1058.

Ewell Vineyard, Barossa Valley Way, Nuriootpa SA 5355. Tel: (08) 8562 4600.

Greenock Creek Vineyard & Cellars, Radford Road, Seppeltsfield SA 5355. Tel: (08) 8562 8103.

Herrmann Holdings, Nuriootpa SA 5355. Tel: (08) 8570 2100.

Hoffmann A & A, Sturt Road, Ebenezer SA 5355. Tel: (08) 8565 6251.

Kaesler Wines, Barossa Valley Way, Nuriootpa SA 5355. Tel: (08) 8562 2711.

Maywald Vineyards, Research Road, Nuriootpa SA 5355. Tel: (08) 8562 1027.

McShane N & J, Moppa Road, Nuriootpa SA 5355. Tel: (08) 8562 3946.

Penfolds Wines, Tanunda Road, Nuriootpa SA 5355. Tel: (08) 8568 9408.

Schiller G, Nuriootpa SA 5355. Tel: (08) 8562 1610.

Schulz R & M, Belvidere Road, Nuriootpa SA 5355. Tel: (08) 8562 3778.

Seppelt Winery, Seppeltsfield Road, Seppeltsfield SA 5355. Tel: (08) 8568 6217.

Viking Wines Estate, Seppeltsfield Road, Marananga SA 5355. Tel: (08) 8562 3842.

Whistler Wines, Seppeltsfield Road, Nuriootpa SA 5355. Tel: (08) 8562 4942.

Wolf Blass Wines, Sturt Highway, Nuriootpa SA 5355. Tel: (08) 8562 1955.

Yunbar Estate, Nuriootpa SA 5355. Tel: 0418 861 337.

Activities while you are there

Wine touring, bushwalking, horse riding and visiting the many small townships in the area.

Berri

Berri is situated 230 km east of Adelaide and lies on the Murray River. The region around Berri is best known for its citrus growing, which includes one of Australia's largest manufacturers of fruit and juice, Berrivale Orchards. Apart from citrus fruits, Berri Estates, founded in 1922, is one of Australia's largest wineries.

Berri's location on the Murray River makes for an interesting stopover, with a number of things to see and do in between working on the orchards and wineries.

Type of work

Berri is a mecca for the working traveller with work available throughout the year. For instance, if picking oranges and mandarines is your thing, you can work from May until August. At this time of year pruning grape vines is also an option. Picking valencia oranges from August through to December follows. Just when you think it's time for a hard earned break, the apricot season kicks in, followed closely by the grape harvest during February until April. Then it's the orange and mandarine season again!

As you can see, if you are looking for an extended period in a beautiful region, Berri just might be a good option, particularly if you also enjoy water sports and bushwalking during your spare time.

Approximate numbers

Every year the Riverland district advertises for workers and in many cases falls short in finding enough workers to pick the fruit. In fact, throughout the year, more than 5000 workers are required in the region.

Accommodation

Berri Riverside Caravan Park. Tel: (08) 8582 3723.

Berri Backpackers. Tel: (08) 8582 3144.

Transport

If you have your own car, head up the Sturt Highway from Adelaide for about 240 km.

Contacts

Tourist Information. Tel: (08) 8584 7919.

Fruit growers

Bariamis Gerries, Cnr Riverview Drive & Chilton Road, Berri SA 5343. Tel: (08) 8582 1564.

Bottrill T & J, Berri SA 5343. Tel: (08) 8583 5354.

Cawse G & E, Fenwick Road, Berri SA 5343. Tel: (08) 8582 1852.

Cornford H & G, 348 Swinstead Road, Winkie SA 5343. Tel: (08) 8583 7355.

Feher L & J, Dalziel Road, Winkie SA 5343. Tel: (08) 8583 7272.

Frost R, Winkie Road, Winkie SA 5343. Tel: (08) 8583 7327.

Lawrie R & M, Sturt Highway, Berri SA 5343. Tel: (08) 8582 1469.

Lippis T & T, Sykes Road, Lyrup SA 5343. Tel: (08) 8583 8262.

Martin K, Katarapko Crescent, Winkie SA 5343. Tel: (08) 8583 7201.

Perres West, Lock 4 Road, Berri SA 5343. Tel: (08) 8582 2975.

Pipinis F, Wilson Street, Berri SA 5343. Tel: (08) 8582 1097.

Plush J & J, Winkie SA 5343. Tel: (08) 8583 7307.

Recchia L, Gallery Terrace, Lyrup SA 5343. Tel: (08) 8583 8216.

Roberts N & I, Chilton Road, Berri SA 5343. Tel: (08) 8582 2637.

Romeo M, Gallery Terrace, Lyrup SA 5343. Tel: (08) 8583 8265.

Schober I & J, Winkie SA 5343. Tel: (08) 8583 7315.

Sukalic I & M, Winkie SA 5343. Tel: (08) 8583 7241.

Tschirpig N & M, Lyrup SA 5343. Tel: (08) 8583 8288.

Vonic R, Tooravale Road, Berri SA 5343. Tel: (08) 8582 1529.

Watts R, Lyrup SA 5343. Tel: (08) 8583 8242.

Zagotsis G & M, JC Smith Road, Berri SA 5343. Tel: (08) 8582 1829.

Activities while you are there

Activities include water sports, visiting wineries and bushwalking in the national parks.

Clare

The town of Clare is approximately one and a half hours drive north of Adelaide, and like the Barossa Valley, is a large producer of world class wine. The area claims to produce the finest riesling in Australia, although the shiraz and other varieties are also suggested as being of a similar class. In all, there are over 30 wineries in the area, with a similar harvest time to the Barossa Valley.

Type of work

The town of Clare is the hub of the Clare Valley wine district and pickers and pruners are required in large numbers for the harvest season from February to April and for off-season pruning from June to August.

Approximate numbers

Over 500 pickers are required during harvest and similar numbers are required over the winter months for pruning.

Accommodation

Clare Caravan Park. Tel: (08) 8842 2724.

Transport

Daily bus service from Adelaide.

Contacts

Tourist Information. Tel: (08) 8842 2131.

Activities while you are there

In mid May Clare is host to the Clare Valley Gourmet Weekend and during ANZAC weekend, the weekend closest to 25 April, the town puts on a Spanish Festival. Apart from the festivals, Clare is a great place to do some bushwalking and horse riding.

Loxton

The town of Loxton is situated 243 km east of Adelaide and has a population of 3380. Established in the 1850s, Loxton is rich in vineyards and fruit orchards. Nestled on the banks of the Murray River, Loxton offers the working traveller time to both work and play, with numerous places to camp and relax along the river.

Type of work

Over 200 fruit orchards in and around Loxton produce a vast number of apples, mandarines, oranges, grapefruit and pears. Like Berri, citrus harvest times offer the best chance of work during the months of May through to February/March, so there is plenty on offer as far as work is concerned. Apart from picking, there are also opportunities in fruit processing during late spring and through the summer months.

The large apple orchards also require workers throughout the year for both harvest picking from February to June and pruning and thinning during off-season.

Approximate numbers

Over 1000 workers are required throughout the year.

Accommodation

Loxton Riverfront Caravan Park. Tel: (08) 8584 7919.

Harvest Trail Lodge. Tel: (08) 8584 5646..

Transport

Daily train service to Loxton from Adelaide.

Contacts

Angas Park Fruit Co, 3 Murray Street, Angaston SA 5353. Tel: (08) 8564 2052.

Nomads on Murray, Sturt Highway, Kingston on Murray SA 5331. Tel: 1800 737378.

R.I.M.S. Personnel, 47 Renmark Avenue, Renmark SA 5341. Tel: (08) 8586 5888.

Solora South, Loxton North SA 5333. Tel: (08) 8584 1322.

Simpson Packing, Gurney Road, Loxton North SA 5333. Tel: (08) 8584 1317.

Yandilla Park, RMB 52, Renmark SA 5341. Tel: (08) 8586 1277.

Fruit growers

Agosta V, Kibby Road, Loxton East SA 5333. Tel: (08) 8584 6913.

Barry M, Edmonson Road, Loxton SA 5333. Tel: (08) 8584 1136.

Biddle B & M, Cutler Road, Loxton North SA 5333. Tel: (08) 8584 1277.

Dowley L, French Road, Loxton North SA 5333. Tel: (08) 8584 1412.

Hentschke T & J, Anderson Road, Loxton North SA 5333. Tel: (08) 8584 1265.

Jaeschke D & J, Loxton SA 5333. Tel: (08) 8582 1129.

Lipman K, New Residence SA 5333. Tel: (08) 8584 9028.

Mangelsdorf P, Fairweather Avenue, Loxton East SA 5333. Tel: (08) 8584 6905.

Pavia Fruitgrowers, 28 Bookpurnong Terrace, Loxton SA 5333. Tel: (08) 8584 9016.

Pontt W, RSD 2013 via Loxton SA 5333. Tel: (08) 8584 9050.

Quirke T & L, Newton Road, Loxton SA 5333. Tel: (08) 8584 6551.

Ruediger B & P, Loxton SA 5333. Tel: (08) 8582 1596.

Swanbury A & M, Loxton SA 5333. Tel: (08) 8584 4769.

Taylor K, Mackey Road, Loxton East SA 5333. Tel: (08) 8584 6951.

Weaver R & M, Balfour-Ogilvy Avenue, Loxton North SA 5333. Tel: (08) 8584 1242.

Wright & Partners, Cutler Road, Loxton North SA 5333. Tel: (08) 8584 1229.

Citrus fruit growers

Barry C, Anderson Road, Loxton North SA 5333. Tel: (08) 8584 1209.

Battams A, Derrick Road, Loxton North SA 5333. Tel: (08) 8584 1226.

Francis K & F, Gordon Road, Loxton East SA 5333. Tel: (08) 8584 6986.

George R & B, New Residence SA 5333. Tel: (08) 8584 9003.

Goldsworthy M, New Residence SA 5333. Tel: (08) 8584 9043.

Huppatz, G & E, Balfour-Ogilvy Avenue, Loxton North SA 5333. Tel: (08) 8584 1429.

Manuel J & J, Middleton Road, Loxton SA 5333. Tel: (08) 8584 7205.

Pfeiler R & R, Briers Road, Loxton North SA 5333. Tel: (08) 8584 1235.

Wilson N & H, Fairweather Avenue, Loxton North SA 5333. Tel: (08) 8584 1484.

Ziersch T & V, Anderson Road, Loxton North SA 5333. Tel: (08) 8584 1238.

Activities while you are there

Bushwalking in nearby national parks, water sports and golf.

Harvest trail - Western Australia

Albany

Albany, 417 km south-east of Perth, is one of Western Australia's most visited tourist destinations. With historic roots dating back to 1826, it is the state's oldest town and attracts many tourists to the buildings that still stand from the early 1800s. Apart from the history, the area around Albany also justifies a visit: the crystal clear water of the Indian Ocean, along with rivers and wineries to the north make Albany an all round favourite.

Type of work

Albany offers the travelling worker many opportunities for work. Grape picking around the area begins in February and lasts until April. During the off season, you may also be lucky and find work pruning vines, which normally takes place over the winter months.

In addition to working in the viticulture industry, hospitality positions during the holiday periods are also possible for those with experience. For example, during Christmas the population of the area can double from 16,400 to over 35,000 which opens many employment opportunities in restaurants, bars and cafes.

Approximate numbers

About 150 vine pruners over winter, over 200 for grape picking and a similar number in hospitality, peaking during school and Christmas holidays.

Accommodation

Albany Backpackers. Tel: (08) 9841 8848.

Albany YHA. Tel: (08) 9841 3949.

Channel Resort. Tel: (08) 9844 8100.

Dog Rock Motel. Tel: (08) 9441 4422.

Emu Beach Caravan Park. Tel: (08) 9844 1147.

Transport

Daily bus service from Perth.

Contacts

Tourist Information Centre. Tel: (08) 9841 1088.

Berry growers

Eden Gate Blueberry Farm, Eden Road, Youngs Siding WA 6330. Tel: (08) 9845 2003.

Handasyde N, Strawberry Farm, Albany WA 6330. Tel: (08) 9844 3419.

Willow Creek Strawberries, Dempster Road, Kalgan WA 6330. Tel: (08) 9846 4300.

Potato farms

Australian Seed Potato Company, Mountain East Road, Bornholm WA 6330. Tel: (08) 9845 1135.

Ayres G, Bornholm South Road, Bornholm WA 6330. Tel: (08) 9845 1014.

Eldridge L & J, RMB 9214, Cuthbert via Albany WA 6330. Tel: (08) 9844 6269.

Vineyards

Bacchus Contracting, Busselton WA 6280. Tel: (08) 9753 1338.

Wagnall's Wines, Chester Pass Road, King River, Albany WA 6330. Tel: (08) 9841 2848.

Zarephath Wines, Moorialup Road, Albany WA 6330. Tel: (08) 9853 1152.

Activities while you are there

There are lots of outdoor activities including fishing, whale watching from July to October, surfing, golfing, visiting nearby wineries and bushwalking in the nearby national park.

Broome

Broome is a subtropical town 2356 km north of Perth. Originally populated by pearlers, Broome's main economic backbone is tourism, with the warm waters of Cable Beach being an iconic draw card for travellers. And where there are tourists, there's work!

Type of work

Hospitality work is the most popular form of earning a dollar in Broome. Due to the isolated position of the town, many workers stay for the dry season and then move on with many heading to south-west Western Australia, which opens new opportunities at the beginning of each dry season for various positions including chefs, waiting staff, kitchen hands, room service and front of house staff, and any other hospitality position you can think of! The dry season lasts from around April through until September/October, so you could plan to do a whole season of work in Broome if you arrive early enough to apply for the better positions.

Approximate numbers

Because of the transient nature of workers in the town, there can be as many as 800 positions available during the dry season. Although the wet season can bring constant rain, keeping tourist numbers down, there is always a need for maintenance staff if you are 'handy' and have good references to show potential employers.

Accommodation

Broome Caravan Park. Tel: (08) 9192 1776.

Kimberley Club Backpackers. Tel: (08) 9192 3233.

Roebuck Bay Backpackers. Tel: (08) 9192 1183.

YHA Broome's Last Resort. Tel: 1800 095 508.

Transport

Bus services operate throughout the week from Perth and Darwin. You can also fly into Broome from the capital cities.

Contacts

Job Network. Tel: (08) 9192 8555.

Kimberley Personnel. Tel: (08) 9193 6631.

SMYL Employment and Training. Tel: (08) 9192 8100.

Tourist Information. Tel: (08) 9192 2222.

Activities while you are there

Relaxing, fishing, reading a good book, horse and camel riding and swimming.

Carnarvon

Carnarvon is 900 km north of Perth and is called the gateway to the north. For the working traveller heading north up the coast it offers some chance of work. In fact, there's something available all year round. With the Gascoyne River acting as an irrigation channel to growers, the amount of produce from the area is increasing every year, which is great news for those seeking seasonal work. The town also has a prawn and fishing industry which provides employment opportunities for the experienced.

Type of work

If you like bananas, you've come to the right place! Jobs in banana plantations are available mainly from June to September. Apart from bananas, Carnarvon is also a producer of various vegetables including capsicums, tomatoes and corn. The peak demand for workers is from June to December.

The fishing industry offers jobs from March to December. The work on boats is physically demanding but it's a great experience for the adventurous. Other work is sometimes available processing the catch, although experience is usually required.

Approximate numbers

Up to 100 workers are needed for the fishing and prawning industry. The vegetable harvests create demand for about 1000 workers while the banana plantation work is available from July to December and the numbers required vary depending on the season.

Accommodation

Carnarvon Backpackers. Tel: (08) 9941 1095.

Carnarvon Beach Holiday Resort. Tel: (08) 9941 2226.

Carnarvon Tourist Centre Caravan Park. Tel: (08) 9941 1438.

Wintersun Caravan Park. Tel: (08) 9941 8150.

Transport

Bus services operate from Perth and Darwin.

Contacts

Carnarvon Growers Association, 69 North West Central Highway, Carnarvon WA 6701.

Mission Employment. Tel: (08) 9941 3848.

Tourist Information. Tel: (08) 9941 1146.

Workbase Employment. Tel: (08) 9941 4577.

Fruit growers

Whitehall-Holla M & K, 'Drummoyne', Carnarvon WA 6701. Tel: (08) 9941 1296.

Banana growers

Garbin I, Lot 72 South River Road, Carnarvon North WA 6701. Tel: (08) 9941 8124.

Westoby Plantation, Robinson Street, Carnarvon North WA 6701. Tel: (08) 9941 8003.

Activities while you are there

Fishing and all other water sports, golfing and scenic drives.

Donnybrook

Donnybrook has a population of 2300 and is 219 km south of Perth. The town is a very popular destination for working travellers, with an abundance of work available for at least eight months of the year. Being in close proximity to Perth, it also allows travellers to drive into Perth and Fremantle for a couple of days well-earned break from harvest work.

Type of work

The main produce in the area is comprised of stone fruits, apples, tomatoes and, to a lesser extent, grapes, although new vines are constantly being planted and therefore more work in this area will become available in the next couple of years. The type of work includes fruit thinning, pruning and picking.

Approximate numbers

The number of workers in the area varies throughout the year, but well over 400 workers are required during the harvest season from October to late May. Therefore, Donnybrook should be a safe bet for those looking for a few months work.

Accommodation

Brooklodge Workstay. Tel: (08) 9731 1520.

Donnybrook Caravan Park. Tel: (08) 9731 1263.

Transport

Daily bus services operate to and from Perth.

Contacts

Cusato A & A, South Western Highway, Donnybrook WA 6239. Tel: (08) 9731 1419.

Delfino G, RMB 624 Boyupbrook Road, Donnybrook WA 6239. Tel: (08) 9731 1169.

Donnybrook District Harvest Office. Tel: (08) 9731 2400.

Jones L, RMB 709 Charlies Creek Road, Donnybrook WA 6239. Tel: (08) 9731 1512.

Keall S & A, 'Queenwood', Donnybrook WA 6239. Tel: (08) 9732 1254.

Licciardello S & R, South Western Highway, Donnybrook WA 6239. Tel: (08) 9731 1289.

Perivale Orchards, The Upper Capel Road, Donnybrook WA 6239. Tel: (08) 9731 6321.

Sunvalley Orchards, RMB 629, Donnybrook WA 6239. Tel: (08) 9731 1174.

Swanto Orchard, 297 South Western Highway, Donnybrook WA 6239. Tel: (08) 9731 1021.

Terace G & Sons, South Western Highway, Donnybrook WA 6239. Tel: (08) 9731 1159.

Workstay Australia, 60 South West Highway, Donnybrook WA 6239. Tel: (08) 9731 2400.

Tourist Information. Tel: (08) 9731 1720.

Activities while you are there

If you happen to be in the area over Easter, check out the Donnybrook Apple Festival. Otherwise, the Preston River offers visitors a number of water sports and recreational activities.

Esperance

Esperance is located 743 km south-east of Perth and has a population of 8500. The beaches are postcard material with white sands, azure water and sheltering islands offshore. Esperance offers inlanders a perfect holiday setting and the working traveller an oasis with a chance to pick up the odd job along the way.

Type of work

If you've always dreamed of shearing sheep, or at least getting close to the action, Esperance offers the working traveller a chance to work during shearing times from July to early November and January to April. It's a good idea to have some experience before enquiring for work. Maybe try a jilleroo/jackeroo course first or gate call offering your time to be trained in return for work.

If lugging fleece ain't your thing, between the months of October and March you may find work in the hospitality industry which thrives during these months. Ensure you arrive with references to increase your chance of finding work.

Two other industries in the area are the grain and fishing industries. Both offer occasional employment, but only for experienced workers. If you do have grain harvest experience, it may also be worth a drive to Salmon Gums and Grass Patch, which are towns located about one hour north of Esperance along the highway to Norseman.

Approximate numbers

Finding work as a shed hand in the shearing sheds or in hospitality is fairly 'hit and miss' in this area, so consider it worth the travel to Esperance to experience the beautiful beaches and friendly community. If you pick up some work, see it as a bonus rather than a necessity, though of course the longer you stay there the more likely you are to pick up work.

Accommodation

Croker's Park Holiday Resort. Tel: (08) 9071 4100.

Esperance Backpackers. Tel: (08) 9071 4724.

Pink Lake Lodge. Tel: (08) 9071 2075.

Transport

You'll need your own transport.

Contacts

Rainbow Labour Contracting, Esperance WA 6450. (08) 9071 6224.

Tourist Information. Tel: (08) 9071 2330.

Shearing contractors

Cronin Shearing Management, Esperance WA 6450. Tel: (08) 9071 5709.

Fang, Lot 12 Burton Street, Esperance WA 6450. Tel: (08) 9071 1128.

Pinchin Shearing, Lot 52 Goldfields Road, Esperance WA 6450. Tel: (08) 9071 1767.

Quay Enterprises, 114 Burton Road, Esperance WA 6450. Tel: (08) 9071 3853.

Willis J, 9 Dempster Street, Esperance WA 6450. Tel: (08) 9071 2078.

Activities while you are there

Esperance itself is a quiet town but activities include water sports, gold fossicking, horse riding, fishing and surfing. A small wind farm can be found nearby on the road to Twilight Beach. The beaches in the area can be very windswept and barren.

Kalgoorlie

In 1893, a young man named Paddy Hannan struck gold. Little did he know that he was sitting on the largest goldfield in Australia! Kalgoorlie is 593 km from Perth and has a population of 26,100.

Apart from gold, Kalgoorlie is also home to a large nickel industry, which started in the 1970s. Today, Kalgoorlie and its neighbouring town Boulder also service outlying pastoral properties and a prospering tourist trade.

Known as the Golden Mile, Kalgoorlie offers the working traveller both an insight into Australia's gold history, as well as an opportunity to pick up casual work, mainly in the hospitality sector.

Type of work
Hospitality work is available in the town from May to September. Positions include chefs, waiters and kitchen hands. Ensure you have references with you and the best method of finding work is to make direct contact with the restaurants, pubs and cafes.

Approximate numbers
About 150 workers are required during the winter months.

Accommodation
Cornwell Hotel. Tel: (08) 9093 2510.

Kalgoorlie Village Caravan Park. Tel: (08) 9093 2780.

Transport
Daily train from Perth.

Contacts
Tourist Information. Tel: (08) 9021 1966.

Activities while you are there
Gold fossicking, golf, mine tours and walks. The Great Gold Festival is held every July and the Spring Festival is held in September.

Katanning

Katanning is a small town with a population of 5100 located 287 km south-east of Perth. It lies in the heart of the most prosperous agricultural region of the state.

Type of work
Like Esperance, without experience in shearing sheds or grain harvesting, jobs may be hard to find, but still worth a look, as you don't have to travel too far to neighbouring fruit and vegetable districts.

Approximate numbers
Variable.

Accommodation

Katanning Caravan Park. Tel: (08) 9821 1066.

Sunbeam Caravan Park. Tel: (08) 9821 2165.

Transport

Daily bus service from Perth.

Contacts

Tourist Information. Tel: (08) 9821 2634.

Shearing contractors

Byrne R & M, 24 Kobeelya Avenue, Katanning WA 6317. Tel: (08) 9821 1502.

Byrne R , 92 Adam Street, Katanning WA 6317. Tel: (08) 9821 4205.

Hanna I & J, 11 Clive Street, Katanning WA 6317. Tel: (08) 9821 5076.

South Shear, 39 Amber Street, Katanning WA 6317. Tel: (08) 9821 4214.

Willey G & K, 29 Broome Street, Katanning WA 6317. Tel: (08) 9821 2225.

Activities while you are there

Activities include scenic drives, tours of the township and swimming.

Kununurra

Kununurra has a population of 4950, and is located 3345 km from Perth. The town has had a short and interesting history, first established in 1961 when the Ord River Scheme was built, which now assists the many growers in the area.

Apart from a vibrant and expanding agricultural industry, there have been diamond finds just south of the town, as well as gas and oil discoveries in the Timor Sea, which has added a new dimension to the town's economy.

Type of work

There is a great deal of opportunity for the working traveller in

Kununurra for most parts of the year, in particular May through until November. Fruit and vegetables are harvested over the entire period and the amount of produce to be harvested sometimes outweighs the number of workers available. The horticulture crops include papaya, citrus, bananas, pumpkins and melons, with the latter being the largest crop.

Approximate numbers

About 500 are needed during the season.

Accommodation

Country Club Hotel. Tel: (08) 9168 1024.

Desert Inn Backpackers Oasis. Tel: (08) 9168 2702.

Kona Lakeside Tourist Park. Tel: (08) 9168 1031.

Kununurra Backpackers. Tel: (08) 9169 1998.

Transport

Bus service between Perth and Darwin.

Contacts

Bardena Farms, 384 Packsaddle Road, Kununurra WA 6743. Tel: 0409 691 505.

Barradale Farm, King Location 277, Kununurra WA 6743. Tel: (08) 9169 1386.

Bluey's Farm, Lot 591 Riverfarm Road, Kununurra WA 6743. Tel: (08) 9168 2177.

Bothkamp Australia Farm, KL 242 Weaber Plains Road, Kununurra WA 6743. Tel: (08) 9168 2037.

Ceres Farm, Lot 3 Packsaddle Road, Kununurra WA 6743. Tel: (08) 9168 1613.

Cummings Bros, Lot 221 River Farm Road, Kununurra WA 6743. Tel: (08) 9168 1196.

Oasis Farms, 241 Stock Route Road, Kununurra WA 6743. Tel: (08) 9169 1282.

Tourist Information. Tel: (08) 9168 1177.

Activities while you are there

Any water sports, including water skiing, fishing, swimming and canoeing. If you are in town around late March, keep your eyes open for the Dam to Dam Dinghy Race.

Manjimup

Manjimup is 310 km south of Perth and offers the working traveller year round work options, not to mention beautiful surroundings, which you have a taste of as you drive under tall timber arches at the entrance to the town.

Many of the tourist attractions centre around timber, and you'll find a drive to the Four Aces worth a look. These are four karri trees believed to be hundreds of years old. There are also many nature walks around the area, as well as manicured wineries with cellar door sales and tasting daily.

Type of work

Manjimup offers a plethora of options, including grape picking from February to April, apples and other fruits from March to June and vegetables all year round.

Approximate numbers

Over 2500 workers are needed every year.

Accommodation

Manjimup Caravan Park. Tel: (08) 9771 2093.

Nyamup Holiday Village. Tel: (08) 9773 1273.

Tobacco Park & Backpackers. Tel: (08) 9772 1228.

Transport

Daily bus service from Perth.

Contacts

Tourist Information. Tel: (08) 9771 1831.

Vegetable growers

Bewray, Lot 11 Morgan Road, Manjimup WA 6258. Tel: (08) 9771 1808.

Wauchope I, Dingup Road, Manjimup WA 6258. Tel: (08) 9772 4208.

Fruit and berry growers

Appletech-Manjimup, Ipsen Street, Manjimup WA 6258. Tel: (08) 9771 1669.

Casuarina Valley Orchard, Etherington Road, Fontyspool WA 6258. Tel: (08) 9771 2241.

Activities while you are there

Apart from being close to the coast, the Manjimup area includes forests and lakes, so there is plenty to do and see, including visiting wineries, bushwalking, water skiing and scenic drives.

Margaret River

The town of Margaret River has a population of 800, but this is a poor indicator of the number of people who reside in the region, both transient and local. The region has become one of the biggest tourist destinations in Western Australia over recent years. This growth has been fuelled by the world class wine that is produced in the area. At last count there were over 200 wineries. The temperate weather is ideal for grape growing and the tourist industry which caters to both a youth market with an abundance of adventure activities and well as those who appreciate a decent drop of wine.

Type of work

Many working travellers venture down to Margaret River during the grape harvest, which runs from February to late April. It's almost a carnival atmosphere, as more than 2500 pickers work the vines from early each morning, and settle into after work yarns at the local pub.

Hospitality employment also becomes an option over the Christmas period, which then flows into harvest time in February. Work includes positions for cooks, chefs, kitchen hands and waiters, but make sure you have relevant references with you when applying for jobs. Winter in Margaret River is peaceful and the weather mild to cool and while work is still available in hospitality, there is less of it.

Approximate numbers

Over 2500 pickers are required for the grape harvest and about 150 pruners are required during winter.

Accommodation

Margaret River Caravan Park. Tel: (08) 9757 2180.

Margaret River Hotel. Tel: (08) 9757 2655.

Wallcliffe Lodge. Tel: (08) 9757 2699.

Transport

Daily bus service from Perth.

Contacts

Tourist Information. Tel: (08) 9757 2911.

Vineyards

Avago Vine Nursery, Margaret River WA 6285. Tel: (08) 9757 2470.

Bacchus Contracting, Busselton WA 6280. Tel: (08) 9753 1338.

Leeuwin Viticultural Contractors, RMB 255A Osmington Road, Margaret River WA 6285. Tel: (08) 9757 4544 or 0417 996 398.

Margaret River Rootstocks, Location 3802, Bussell Highway, Margaret River WA 6285. Tel: (08) 9757 2239.

Redgate Wines, Cnr Caves Road & Boodjidup Road, Margaret River WA 6285. Tel: (08) 9757 6488.

Rockfield Estate Vineyard, Rosa Glen Road, Margaret River WA 6285. Tel: (08) 9757 5006.

Rosa Park Vineyard, Blain Road, Rosa Brook WA 6285. Tel: (08) 9757 5058.

Rosabrook Estate Wines, Rosa Brook Road, Margaret River WA 6285. Tel: (08) 9757 2286.

Rudrum's Nursery, Osmington WA 6285. Tel: (08) 9757 8103.

The Berry Farm, RMB 222 Bessell Road, Margaret River WA 6285. Tel: (08) 9757 5054.

Voyager Estate Vineyard, Stevens Road, Margaret River WA 6285. Tel: (08) 9757 6449.

Xanadu Wines, Terry Road, Margaret River WA 6285. Tel: (08) 9757 2581.

Activities while you are there

There are activities for young and old. For starters, try some abseiling, caving and bushwalking. If you've still got the energy, why not do some rock climbing or fishing, and visit some of the 200 wineries in the region. In fact, for those with discerning palates, make your way to the Margaret River Food and Wine Festival held at the beginning of harvest in February each year. Finally, Margaret River is the home of a big wave surf classic held each November, a tribute to the great surf in the area.

Pemberton

Pemberton has a population of just 870 and is located 344 km south of Perth. Typical of the south-west corner of Western Australia, Pemberton is surrounded by soaring forests of marri, jarrah and karri. You can view these forests in comfort on the restored Pemberton Tramway.

Type of work

Pemberton is a short drive from Margaret River and offers the working traveller several harvest opportunities, particularly during the autumn and early winter months from April to June. Apart from apples, grapes are also grown in the district, although not to the same extent as around Margaret River, but worth a look during the harvest which begins late summer and pruning during the winter months.

Approximate numbers

Apple picking is undertaken from February to April and the number of pickers varies depending on the time of the season and how successful the season has been. About 100 workers are needed for grape picking.

Accommodation

Pemberton Backpackers. Tel: (08) 9776 1105.

Pemberton Caravan Park. Tel: (08) 9776 1300.

Pemberton Hotel. Tel: (08) 9776 1017.

Pemberton YHA. Tel: (08) 9776 1153.

Transport

Daily bus service from Perth.

Contacts

Tourist Information. Tel: (08) 9776 1133.

Apple and pear growers

Casuarina Valley Orchard, Etherington Road, Fontyspool WA 6258. Tel: (08) 9771 2241.

Other fruit growers

Avonova, Old Vasse Road, Pemberton WA 6260. Tel: (08) 9776 1332.

O'Connell P & K, Erinscott Berry Farm, Cnr Robinson & Abbott Streets, WA 6260. Tel: (08) 9776 1080.

Activities while you are there

Pemberton offers many activities including bushwalking, fishing, horse riding and wineries.

Harvest trail - Northern Territory

Alice Springs

Alice Springs, originally known as Stuart, is 1513 km south of Darwin and is the centre point of Australia. The 'Alice', as it is affectionately known, is a great base for exploring the Red Centre and is the main departure point to the famous Uluru (Ayers Rock) and Kata Tjuta (The Olgas) to the south-west.

Type of work

With a thriving tourist population, Alice Spring itself offers general work opportunities in the town, including work in retail, construction and even in aged-care and disability support. It is definitely worth visiting the personnel agencies to see what work is available at the time. The feedback from many working travellers during the writing of this book suggests that Alice Springs is underrated as an area to find jobs. See the chapter on resorts for details on more work opportunities in the Red Centre.

The area is also home to a medium sized table grape industry. Although you'll require your own transport, a trip to Ti Tree which is approximately 180 km north of Alice Springs, may be worth the effort for picking work.

Approximate numbers

For work in Alice Springs itself, numbers are hard to quantify, but generally speaking, a variety of work is available year round for those eager to seek it in both hospitality and general employment.

Ti Tree can offer harvest work from October to December, although be prepared to use your own transport. In a good season around 100 to 200 grape pickers are required and off-season work such as pruning can also be available between May and July.

Accommodation

Alice Springs Backpackers Resort, 94 Todd Street, Alice Springs NT 0870. Tel: (08) 8952 2308.

Alice's Secret Travellers Inn, 6 Khalick Street, Alice Springs NT 0870. Tel (08) 8952 8855

Annie's Place, 4 Traeger Avenue, Alice Springs NT 0870. Tel (08) 8952 8686 or 1800 783 633

Elke's Backpackers Resort, 39 Gap Road, Alice Springs NT 0870. Tel (08) 8952 1545

G'day Mate Park, Palm Circuit, Alice Springs. Tel: 8952 9589.

Melanka Backpackers, 94 Todd Street, Alice Springs NT 0870. Tel (08) 8952 4744 or 1800 815 066

Ossie's Hostel, Cnr Lindsay Avenue and Warburton Street, Alice Springs NT 0870. Tel 1800 628 211

Pioneer YHA, Cnr Parsons Street & Leichhardt Terrace, Alice Springs NT 0870. Tel: (08) 8952 8855.

Red Centre Resort, North Stuart Highway, Alice Springs NT 0870. Tel: (08) 8952 8955.

Stuart Lodge YWCA, Stuart Terrace, Alice Springs NT 0870. Tel: (08) 8952 1894.

Toddy's Backpackers Resort, 41 Gap Road, Alice Springs NT 0870. Tel: (08) 8952 1322.

Transport

Road coaches operate between Adelaide and Darwin or you can travel by train from Adelaide on The Ghan.

Contacts

Divoli Farms, Ti Tree via Alice Springs NT 0872.

Table Grape Growers of Australia, Alice Springs NT 0872. Tel: (08) 8956 9744.

The Desert Fruit Co., Alice Springs NT 0870. Tel: (08) 8952 2425.

Tourist Information: (08) 8952 5199.

Activities while you are there

Activities include horse riding, camel riding, hot-air ballooning and bushwalking in numerous national parks in the area. If you walk without a local guide, great care needs to be taken, especially in the hotter months. Always have a hat and carry plenty of water and never stray far from the beaten track. As far as events are concerned, there is something going on all year it seems. As a sample, the Bantail Muster with a parade of floats is worth a look in May, while the famous Henley-On-Todd takes place in September: a boat regatta in a dry river!

Darwin

Darwin has a population of around 100,000 and is known as one of the most cosmopolitan cities in Australia. It is a tourist destination during the dry winter months, while during the summer wet season it becomes very humid and wet and rather uncomfortable for those not used to it.

Type of work

During the dry months Darwin draws tourists, both domestic and international, in large numbers. It therefore offers opportunities in the hospitality industry during the peak season, which normally runs from April to October.

The mango industry is extremely healthy in the area and many workers are required during harvest which starts in September and finishes sometime in December, before the wet season seriously sets in. The industry is still developing, with plantations on the increase and therefore additional work will be available in the future in and around the Darwin area.

Approximate numbers

The hospitality industry requires anywhere between 400 and 600 workers during the dry season while the mango harvest requires more than 800 workers.

Accommodation

Darwin City YHA, 69 Mitchell Street, Darwin NT 0800. Tel: (08) 8981 3995.

Frogshollow Backpackers, 27 Lindsay Street, Darwin NT 0800. Tel: (08) 8941 2600.

Nomads Backpackers, 69a Mitchell Street, Darwin NT 0800. Tel: (08) 8941 9722.

YMCA, The Esplanade, Darwin NT 0800. Tel: (08) 8981 8377.

Transport
A daily coach operates from most capital cities.

Contacts
Employment National, 5C Coolalinga Shopping Centre, Coolalinga NT 0836. Tel: 1300 720 126 (during the mango harvest season).

Tourist Information. Tel: (08) 8981 4300.

Activities while you are there
From a historical point of view, check out Government House, built in 1883, while the Darwin Hotel, built in the same year, offers the working traveller a chance to chat to locals while enjoying a cool ale.

Outside of town, the World Heritage listed Kakadu National Park is a must-see attraction, as is Litchfield National Park, which is a great place for a walk in nature.

Katherine

Katherine is located 321 km south-east of Darwin and has a population of 11,200. It sits beside the Katherine River and is a training base for the Royal Australian Air Force (RAAF). Katherine is the perfect place to learn about Aboriginal culture and a visit to the Aboriginal Cultural Centre is a must for visitors.

Apart from touring the historical buildings of Katherine you can also visit Katherine Gorge, which is located in the Nitmiluk National Park 30 km east of the town. The Cutta Cutta Caves are about 20 km south of the town and can be viewed on guided tours.

Type of work
Katherine has a well developed mango industry, which requires workers from September to November. Other major crops include watermelons, which are harvested from October to early December.

However, the majority of pickers come to the area seeking work in the large mango industry.

Approximate numbers

Between 400 and 800 workers are required for the mango harvest and a smaller number of are required for the watermelon harvest.

Accommodation

Kookaburra Backpackers, Lindsay Street, Katherine NT 0851. Tel: (08) 8971 0257.

Palm Court Backpackers, Cnr Third & Giles Streets, Katherine NT 0850. Tel: (08) 8972 2722.

Transport

Buses travel to and from Katherine, Alice Springs and Darwin.

Contacts

Employment National, 1/17 First Street, Katherine NT 0851. Tel: (08) 8973 1081.

Mango growers

Golding I & M, Lot 3258 Fox Street, Katherine NT 0850. Tel: (08) 8971 7414.

Manbulloo Mangoes, Victoria Highway, Katherine NT 0850. Tel: (08) 8972 2590.

Activities while you are there

As mentioned above, the Katherine Gorge is definitely something worthwhile seeing. If you are in town during July, join in the festivity of the Katherine Show and Rodeo. Other activities include treating yourself to a boat cruise, going fishing or for a bushwalk through spectacular wilderness.

Resort work

Although the majority of employment listings in this book cover harvest work, there is ample opportunity to travel around Australia working in bars, restaurants and, as you'll find in this chapter, resorts.

Resorts in Australia cater for a range of clientele, from families to conference delegates, and cover a range of styles from moderately priced operations to all inclusive, five-star hospitality that only the very wealthy can afford. Some of Australia's top shelf resorts cater for Hollywood stars and business magnates from around the world, who seek the refuge of exclusive resorts on isolated tropical islands (gin and tonic on tap of course!).

This chapter only covers the tip of the iceberg in respect to the total number of resorts around Australia that provide employment opportunities for the working traveller.

In nearly all cases you will need some experience and/or qualifications to work in the resorts, particularly in the hospitality areas. However, housekeeping, garbage collecting and other fairly low skilled work can be sought without the need for much experience. Importantly, if you have a trade qualification such as plumbing or carpentry, other work opportunities will come your way as resorts need to constantly maintain and regularly upgrade their facilities. Resorts on the Great Barrier Reef islands seem to be forever changing ownership and with each new owner comes a major renovation. And each renovation requires lots of tradespeople.

One final point to make about resort work: it is <u>not</u> a holiday! Personnel managers in the resort industry commonly remark that many employees lose their job within first two weeks of starting work because they slip into holiday mode. Always follow the conditions of employment, which may for instance include free use of the facilities, but <u>only during your time off</u>. If you stick to the rules, you'll find yourself having the best of both worlds. While working on the job, self discipline is a great asset.

Good luck in hunting for resort work, whether it is in the Red Centre, on the Reef or on the ski slopes in wintertime!

Queensland

Bedarra Island

Where is it?
Bedarra Island is also a member of the Family group of islands and is located approximately seven km off the coast of Mission Beach in Far North Queensland, approximately half way between Townsville and Cairns. Dunk Island, the most famous of the nearby islands, is only a 15 minute boat ride away.

Getting there
You can reach Bedarra via Dunk Island by a 15 minute trip on the resort's launch. The most popular form of transport to Dunk Island is a 45 minute flight on an 18 seat Twin Otter Aircraft from Cairns. Macair Airlines operates three return flights each day. Resort employees are eligible for discount tickets and bookings are made through the resort.

Alternatively, Dunk Island Express (Tel: (07) 4068 8310) operates a 15 minute water taxi transfer from Wongaling Beach, near Mission Beach, six times daily. The Quickcat (Tel: (07) 4068 7289) operates a 30 minute daily catamaran transfer from Clump Point. Call the relevant operator for schedule times and fares. Car storage is available in an outdoor area with Dunk Island Express.

A weekly barge operated on behalf of the resort transports all operating supplies from Cairns and resort staff are welcome to use this service to transport their belongings to the island at no charge.

About the resort
Bedarra Island caters for a select clientele. No more than 15 couples at any one time are on the island. Bedarra prides itself on being a boutique style resort catering for those who wish to escape the pressures of everyday life. The emphasis is on relaxation and

indulgence, supported by attentive, unobtrusive and friendly service. The tariff includes all meals and an open bar.

Approximately 50 per cent of guests are Australian and 50 per cent international. Bedarra has a high ratio of return guests. The resort does not cater for children under 16 years of age.

Peak season

The peak season for the resort is from July through to December.

Working on Bedarra Island

There are a range of roles available, with the most common opportunities arising in housekeeping, restaurant and kitchen work. Due to the small number of staff there are often opportunities for multi-skilled employees who can work in a variety of positions.

The resort looks for people with initiative, who are well presented, have impeccable personal grooming, outstanding social skills, strong attention to detail and the ultimate discretion.

Number of employees

There are approximately 22 staff working and living on Bedarra Island.

Living on Bedarra Island

The staff village on Bedarra Island offers air-conditioned, fully furnished accommodation on a twin share basis with separate shower and toilet. Supervisors and managers are provided with single accommodation including a private bathroom. A communal staff dining area offers TV, video, fridge, microwave, dishwashing facilities and laundry area complete with dryers. Other social facilities include a computer with internet access, pool table and stereo. New release videos are provided. Employees are charged a nominal amount for accommodation, currently this is around $36 per week.

Contact details

Visit the Voyages Hotels and Resorts website, where you will find an online employment application form to fill-in. Website: www.voyages.com.au/corporate/careers.

Brampton Island

Where is it?

Brampton Island is located in the Cumberland group of islands, 32 km north-east of Mackay at the southern entrance to the Whitsunday Passage. Mackay is 978 km north of Brisbane and 360 km north of Rockhampton. The closest Whitsunday Islands is Lindeman Island. Brampton's sister island, Carlisle Island, is only 300 metres to the east and is easily reached by boat or by walking across the sandbar during low tide.

Getting there

Macair Airlines flies an 18 seater Twin Otter aircraft from Mackay to Brampton Island three times per day. Flights from Hamilton Island are scheduled three times per week. Resort employees are eligible for discounted tickets and bookings may be made through the resort. A number of charter companies also offer flights to the island on demand. Discounted rates are available to resort staff.

The MV Heron II, Brampton's own launch service, leaves Mackay outer harbour at 11.30 a.m. each day except Tuesday and Wednesday. The launch leaves Brampton for the return trip to Mackay at approximately 1.00 p.m. The trip takes one hour each way and resort staff travel free. Mackay is a 90 minute flight or a ten hour drive from Brisbane.

A weekly barge operated on behalf of the resort transports all operating supplies from Mackay and resort staff are welcome to use this service to transport their belongings to the island at no charge.

About the resort

Almost entirely national park, Brampton has seven glorious golden sandy beaches and its own coral reef. Kangaroos and exotic species of birds live in and around the resort in unspoiled native bushland.

The nightly tariff includes all meals as well as many activities including non-motorised water sports, tennis, mini golf and walks.

The resort represents very good value for money, with all meals and most activities included in the tariff. This tends to attract a very strong domestic market mainly from Brisbane, Sydney and Melbourne. The resort is very popular with couples of all ages, particularly those in the 25 to 35 year age range and those over 45. School holiday periods attract a family market, although this trend is changing as the resort does not offer a kids' club facility.

Peak season

Peak season is generally from July to November. The resort is also busy during the festive season and the Easter holidays.

Working on Brampton Island

The resort offers employment opportunities in a broad range of areas such as housekeeping, front office work, and food and beverage work. Being a remote and self contained location, there are also positions available in non-hospitality roles including those for nurses, massage therapists, retail attendants, mechanics, electricians, plumbers and carpenters. The resort also has a large team of water sports, activities and entertainment officers to keep things rolling along.

Number of employees

There are approximately 85 staff working and living on Brampton Island.

Living on Brampton Island

Brampton Island Resort offers a number of staff accommodation options. Most staff live in three blocks of accommodation that adjoin the national park. Two staff members generally share a room with a bathroom between every two rooms. All rooms are fully furnished and have ceiling fans. Accommodation for department heads is in small semi-detached units, some boasting great ocean or national park views, and all containing their own cooking facilities. Employees are charged a nominal amount for accommodation, currently around $36 per week.

Contact details

Visit the Voyages Hotels and Resorts website, where you will find an online employment application form to fill-in. Website: www.voyages.com.au/corporate/careers.

Coconut Beach Resort

Where is it?

Coconut Beach Resort is located in the heart of Cape Tribulation in Far North Queensland and is nestled between two world heritage areas: the Great Barrier Reef and the Daintree National Park, approximately 140 km north of Cairns and 75 km south of Cooktown. The drive from Cairns is about two and a half hours.

Getting there

The most popular means of reaching Cape Tribulation is from Cairns by car. Alternatively, there are coach transfers available from Cairns departing twice daily.

About the resort

Coconut Beach Resort has 66 guest rooms in four-star comfort amid wild surrounds and private rainforest views with Coconut beach in walking distance.

Coconut Beach Resort attracts a wide range of people with an interest in eco-tourism with a touch of comfort. Activities at the resort include self-guided rainforest walks through the grounds and adjacent rainforest and an opportunity for swimming both in the resort pools and nearby Coconut Beach.

Peak season

Peak season is from June to January.

Working on Coconut Beach Resort

Coconut Beach Resort requires a diverse range of staff including activity attendants, electricians, water sports staff, food and beverage staff, cleaners and carpenters.

Contact details

In February 2007 this property was purchased from Voyages Hotels and Resorts by Ocean Hotels. Go to www.capetribulationresorts.com.au. Here you'll find information about employment. Ocean Hotels also has Ferntree Forest Lodge among some other properties in Queensland which may also provide job opportunities.

Dunk Island

Where is it?

Dunk Island is a member of the Family group of islands, situated 4 km off the coast of Mission Beach, in Far North Queensland, midway between Cairns and Townsville.

Getting there

The most popular means of reaching Dunk Island is from Cairns via a 45 minute flight on an 18 seat Twin Otter aircraft. Three return flights are operated each day by Macair Airlines. Resort employees are eligible for discounted tickets and bookings may be made through the resort.

Alternatively, you can travel with Dunk Island Express (Tel: (07) 4068 8310) which operates a 15 minute water taxi transfer from Wongaling Beach near Mission Beach six times daily. The Quickcat (Tel: (07) 4068 7289) operates a 30 minute daily catamaran transfer from Clump Point. Call the relevant operator for up-to-date schedule times and fares. Car storage in an outdoor area is available with Dunk Island Express.

About the resort

Dunk Island is a tropical rainforest island off the coast of Far North Queensland. With a wide range of adventure and luxury activities, there is something for everyone! The 147 guest rooms on Dunk Island are nestled in tropical gardens or are located on the beach with magnificent ocean views. The resort has two restaurants, three bars, a six-hole golf course, three tennis courts, a squash court, gym, two swimming pools and its own farm.

With high peaked mountains, dense rainforests, golden beaches and the surrounding sea, it is no wonder that Dunk Island is marketed as 'Australia's Most Beautiful Rainforest Island'.

Dunk Island attracts a wide range of people, from honeymoon couples and young families to mature couples and elderly tour groups. It attracts 50 per cent domestic and 50 per cent international guests. The resort also has a Kids' Club and attracts a strong family market during Australian school holidays.

Peak season
Peak season is from June to January.

Working on Dunk Island
Dunk Island requires a diverse range of staff including activity attendants, electricians, water sports staff, food and beverage staff, cleaners and carpenters.

Number of employees
There are approximately 160 staff working and living on Dunk Island.

Living at Dunk Island Resort
All staff live on Dunk Island in the staff village. Twin share rooms include a bathroom, fridge, basic furnishings and a veranda or patio. Each block or accommodation area has its own laundry, clothes dryers and ironing facilities. Employees are charged a nominal amount for accommodation, currently about $28 per week.

A weekly barge operated on behalf of the resort transports all operating supplies from Cairns. Resort staff are welcome to use this service to transport their belongings to the island at no charge.

Contact details
Visit the Voyages Hotels and Resorts website, where you will find an online employment application form to fill-in. Website: www.voyages.com.au/corporate/careers.

Great Keppel Island

Where is it?
Great Keppel Island is 55 km from Rockhampton and 15 km east of Rosslyn Bay, off the Capricorn Coast of Queensland.

Getting there
The island can be reached by a 15 minute flight on Sunstate Airlines from Rockhampton, which is itself served from major capital cities by scheduled domestic airline services. Alternatively, you can travel to the island by launch from Rosslyn Bay, a 25 minute trip.

About the resort

Great Keppel Island Resort has been recently taken over by the Accor Hotel Group and will be branded under their Mercure banner.

The resort caters for both families and business. Most activities are included in the rate and conference facilities are suitable for small and large groups.

Working on Great Keppel Island

The normal resort jobs are available, as well as other work involved in the maintenance of the island.

Number of employees

At the time of writing, there were approximately 80 people working at Contiki Resort Great Keppel Island, however this figure changes with seasonality with the peak guest period being over the summer.

Living on Great Keppel Island

All staff live on the resort and a small deduction in salary covers both food and accommodation in either single and shared rooms.

Contact details

Contiki Holidays - Travel House, 35 Grafton Street, Woollahra NSW 2025. Tel: (02) 9511 2200. Email: gkihr @gkeppel.com.au. Website: www.gkeppel.com.au.

Hamilton Island

Where is it?

Hamilton Island is situated in the heart of the Whitsunday Islands and is one of 74 tropical islands that lie between the Queensland coast and the Great Barrier Reef.

Getting there

As the largest inhabited island in the Whitsunday group, Hamilton Island is the only island with an airport catering for direct commercial and charter flights. It is serviced by at least 48 flights a week by Qantas and Sunstate Airlines, including direct flights from Melbourne, Sydney, Brisbane, Cairns and Townsville with convenient connections to domestic and international airports.

About the resort

Over 80 per cent of Hamilton Island has been carefully preserved in its natural state so that visitors can continue to enjoy the pristine beauty of the island's fabulous beaches, unspoilt nature trails and secluded hideaways.

Over recent years, Hamilton Island Limited has invested almost $56 million in refurbishing and upgrading existing features as well as creating new facilities. The resort offers an off-shore village complex that caters to overseas visitors and the crews of ocean going yachts. It is a bustling resort with sporting facilities on land and sea, nightly entertainment, launch and yacht charters and a choice of restaurants.

Working on Hamilton Island

Typical resort work is available including food and beverage work, front of house duties and housekeeping. The human resources manager stresses a need for employees who can offer a minimum six month commitment to working on the resort.

Number of employees

The resort has a staff of 750.

Living on Hamilton Island

Twin share accommodation is provided for staff with $25 per week deducted from an employee's salary to cover board only. Meals cost extra so employees should bring their own cooking gear and it'll be a bit cheaper if you can purchase your food on the mainland.

Contact details

Email: hr@hamiltonisland.com.au. Website: www.hamilton.island.com.au.

Hayman Island Resort

Where is it?

Hayman Island—the most northerly island in the Whitsunday group—is 400 ha in area and eight km in circumference. Its tallest peak stands 250 m above sea level. Other islands and the mainland can be seen from Hayman Island and are reached by boat or yacht.

About the resort

The resort has 234 rooms and caters for holiday makers wanting a break, honeymooners, weddings and conferences.

Working on Hayman Island Resort

Hayman Island offers much more in the way of employment than most other resorts, due to its self sufficiency, for example the requirement to treat its own sewage. The resort therefore has a greater need for people with trades.

Number of employees

The resort employs a staff of 500.

Living on Hayman Island

Accommodation is provided for staff, and 95 per cent of staff live on the island. Accommodation is varied depending on how long you've worked at the resort, and what you do. Entry level accommodation includes a shared room for two people and is provided free, along with three meals a day.

Contact details

Hayman Island Resort, Great Barrier Reef QLD 4801. Tel: (07) 4940 1234. Recruitment Hotline: (07) 4740 1133. Fax: (07) 4940 1567. Email: recruit@hayman.com.au. Website: www.hayman.com.au.

Heron Island

Where is it?

Heron Island Resort is a coral cay situated on the southern end of the Great Barrier Reef. The island, within the Capricorn Bunker group of islands, is located 70 km off the city of Gladstone on the central Queensland coast. Gladstone is 600 km north of Brisbane.

Heron Island is 17 ha in area, 1.7 km in circumference and no more than five m above sea level at its highest point. The island is a national park and bird sanctuary. A University of Queensland research station and a National Parks and Wildlife ranger station are also located on the island.

Getting there

The most popular method of transportation to Heron Island

is the catamaran service operated by the resort which departs from the Gladstone marina at 11 a.m. daily and takes approximately two hours each way. Travel is free for resort employees.

Marine Helicopters also operates a heli-transfer to Heron Island and resort employees are eligible for standby rates.

There are several options available for travel to and from Gladstone: Qantas operates flights to Gladstone via Brisbane with a flight time of approximately 80 minutes. A courtesy coach departs Gladstone airport each morning for transfer to Gladstone Marina. This connects with the Heron Island catamaran service.

The Queensland Rail tilt train departs from Brisbane every day except Saturday at 10.30 a.m. and arrives in Gladstone at 4.20 p.m. Greyhound Australia operates regular bus services to Gladstone from Sydney and Brisbane. The approximate travel time from Brisbane is ten hours. The drive from Brisbane to Gladstone is approximately six hours. If you have a car there are several options for storage in Gladstone.

A weekly barge operated on behalf of the resort transports all operating supplies from Gladstone and resort staff are welcome to use this service to transport their belongings to the island at no charge.

About the resort

At Heron Island the reef actually starts at the end of the beach. You just step off the white sands, grab your snorkelling gear and start exploring the magical underwater world of the Great Barrier Reef.

Guest accommodation at Heron Island Resort ranges from attractive Reef or Heron Suites to spacious Point Suites and a Beach House. Unlike many other resorts, meals are included in the tariff, including the spectacular Saturday night seafood smorgasbord.

The resort offers guests casual carefree days to explore the reef through scuba diving and snorkelling expeditions, or in a semi-submersible. There are also guided reef walks at low tide and informative island walks through the forest.

The resort attracts dive enthusiasts and couples with an interest in nature. The majority of guests are between the ages of 30 and 65. Approximately 55 per cent of the clientele are international travellers with the majority coming from the US, UK and Europe. The remaining 45 per cent are generally from the east coast of Australia.

Peak season

Peak occupancy periods at the resort are from September through to February. The Easter holidays are also popular.

Working on Heron Island

Heron Island Resort offers employment opportunities in the following areas: food and beverage, boating, diving, housekeeping, front office, kitchen, maintenance, nursing, leisure activities and retail.

Number of employees

There are about 115 employees working and living on island.

Living on Heron Island

The staff residential area is located in the centre of the island. Staff accommodation is generally provided on a twin share basis, with single rooms for supervisory staff. Accommodation consists of blocks of four rooms, each with its own entrance and small balcony. The rooms are basic, and staff are encouraged to bring decorative and personal items to help make them feel at home.

The amenities block, located within the staff village, provides the majority of Heron Island staff with communal shower and toilets facilities. Laundry facilities are provided at the main amenities block.

Staff recreation on the island is organised and funded by the social club. An in-house video system is connected to each of the staff rooms. Employees are charged a nominal amount for accommodation, currently around $36 per week.

Contact details

Visit the Voyages Hotels and Resorts website, where you will find an online employment application form to fill-in. Website: www.voyages.com.au/corporate/careers.

Lizard Island

Where is it?

Lizard Island is located right on the Great Barrier Reef, approximately 37 km off the coast of Queensland, 240 km north of

Cairns. In addition to the resort, there is also a research station on the island, operated by the Australian Museum from Sydney, where research is conducted into the reef and its marine life.

Getting there

The island is a one-hour flight from Cairns and is serviced by scheduled daily flights. Resort staff receive discounted rates with Macair Airlines (www.macair.com.au) and a number of charter companies.

About the resort

Lizard Island Resort is Australia's northernmost island resort. It is world famous for its enviable position on the Great Barrier Reef, its spectacular coral gardens directly offshore and 24 secluded white sandy beaches.

There are just 40 villas and suites. The nightly tariff includes all meals and many activities including guided walks and a variety of water sports such as sailing catamarans, sailboarding, sea kayaking and snorkelling.

The resort caters to a discerning upmarket clientele, primarily couples in search of active indulgence. A high proportion are return guests. International visitors comprise approximately 50 per cent of all guests. The resort does not cater for children under 10 years of age. The most popular guest activity is snorkelling or diving on the Great Barrier Reef.

Peak season

Peak season is from July to November. The period from late September to early November is particularly busy due to the marlin fishing season, which takes place in the surrounding waters. The marlin season attracts well-to-do people from around the world.

Working on Lizard Island

The resort offers employment opportunities in a broad range of areas including traditional hospitality roles such as housekeeping, front office staff and food and beverage staff. Being a remote and self contained location, there are often employment openings in non-hospitality areas including nurses, dive instructors, mechanics, electricians, plumbers and carpenters. If you're interested in these areas you may need to put your name down for a future vacancy. Applicants in these areas need to have plenty of experience and be able to work on their own.

Number of employees

There are approximately 85 staff working and living on Lizard Island.

Living on Lizard Island

Lizard Island Resort offers a number of staff accommodation options, all modern and well maintained. Rooms are fully furnished and have air-conditioning. Staff generally receive their own room.

Gekko Hill consists of a variety of free standing and duplex buildings. All rooms have a private bathroom. Accommodation in this village has recently been refurbished and repainted.

Goanna Flats consist of three blocks each containing eight rooms and four bathrooms. All rooms have their own covered decking with a fan. The Department Head Village, which consists of relocated guest rooms, all quite large and extremely modern, is also located at Goanna Flats. Employees are charged a nominal amount for accommodation, currently this is around $45 per week.

A fortnightly barge operated on behalf of the resort transports all operating supplies from Cairns, and resort staff are welcome to use this service to transport their belongings to the island at no charge.

Contact details

Visit the Voyages, Hotels and Resorts website, where you will find an online employment application form to fill-in. Website: www.voyages.com.au/corporate/careers.

Novotel Beachcomber – Surfers Paradise

Where is it?

Novotel Beachcomber is located in the heart of Surfers Paradise on the Gold Coast, south-east of Brisbane.

Getting there

Fly into Coolangatta Airport and take a bus northwards on the Pacific Highway or alternatively, drive right to the door step!

About the resort

Located only a few minutes walk from Main Beach, this hotel has a licensed restaurant, bar, two heated swimming pools, spa, tennis court, gym and barbecue.

The resort caters for family and business markets.

Working at Novotel Beachcomber Resort

Typical resort work is available including food and beverage work, administration and front of house duties.

Number of employees

The resort employs a staff of 70.

Living at Novotel Beachcomber Resort

No accommodation is provided for staff at the resort, although reasonably priced accommodation is available in and around Surfers Paradise.

Contact details

Novotel Beachcomber Resort, 18 Hanlan Street, Surfers Paradise QLD 4217. Tel: (07) 5570 1000. Website: www.accorhotels.com.au/corporate/job_opportunities.asp.

Novotel Daydream Island Resort

Where is it?

Daydream Island is in the Whitsunday group of islands and close to the mainland being only just five km from Shute Harbour.

Getting there

Daydream Island is serviced by Hamilton Island Airport and Prosperpine airport. From Hamilton Island, it is a 45 minute trip across the Whitsunday Passage, or from Prosperpine airport, catch a coach to Shute Harbour then take a 15 minute boat trip to the island.

About the resort

Newly renovated with an emphasis on health and well being, this island resort is offering a new way for guests to revitalise themselves in luxury.

Daydream Island has all the usual attractions for families and conference delegates, but has an added edge for those seeking natural therapies in beautiful beach surroundings and the warm Queensland sun.

Working on Daydream Island
Normal resort work is available as well as work for natural therapists who are required during busy periods.

Number of employees
210 to 250 workers are employed at any one time.

Living on Daydream Island
There is accommodation for 100 staff on the resort. The remainder stay at Airlie Beach, which is connected to the island by eight boat trips a day.

Contact details
Human Resources Department, PMB 22, Mackay QLD 4740. Tel: (07) 4948 8488. Email: recruitment@daydream.net.au. Website: www.daydream.net.au.

Novotel Palm Cove Resort

Where is it?
Palm Cove resort is located 25 km north of Cairns and 15 minutes from Cairns airport.

Getting there
By air to Cairns international airport or by car to the resort.

About the resort
Palm Cove Resort is set in 45 ha of lush tropical gardens close to both the beach and the village of Palm Cove. The resort caters to both families and business. The facilities offer child-minding facilities for young children and a Kids' Club for the older ones during the day and evening, which allows for a restful time for exhausted parents. In addition, the resort has conference facilities for small and large business conferences, and recreational facilities to keep both families and business bods occupied during their time away from the conference rooms.

Working at Palm Cove Resort
Typical resort work is available including that for food and beverage staff, front of house staff, maintenance workers and recreation officers.

Number of employees
Over 200 staff are employed at the resort.

Living at Palm Cove
There are no accommodation facilities for staff. However, the surrounding area of Palm Cove and Cairns has budget accommodation in close proximity to the resort.

Contact details
Coral Coast Drive, Palm Cove QLD 4879. Tel: (07) 4059 1234 Website: www.accorhotels.com.au/corporate/job_opportunities.asp.

Orpheus Island Resort

Where is it?
Orpheus Island is 190 km south of Cairns.

Getting there
The island is reached by seaplane, a 60 minute trip from Cairns, or a 25 minute trip from Townsville.

About the resort
Orpheus Island Resort is privately owned and situated in one of several sheltered bays on the western side of the island. It offers guests privacy, sophistication and total relaxation in an unspoiled environment. This idyllic serene hideaway caters to a maximum of 74 guests. Day trippers are not permitted and the resort does not cater for children under 15 years of age.

Activities on the island include reef cruises, game fishing, water skiing, scuba diving, snorkelling and tennis.

In the 1930s Orpheus attracted guests seeking sanctuary from the frenzy of the outside world. Actress Vivienne Leigh and American western novelist Zane Grey were among the first to visit the island more than half a century ago. Today, Orpheus remains a sanctuary from the daily grind of modern hectic life.

Working on Orpheus Island
Typical resort work is available. As the resort is totally self-sufficient it also has work for people with a trade and engineering background.

Number of employees
The resort has a staff of 40.

Living on Orpheus Island
All staff accommodation is on-site with meals provided at a cost of around $92 per week.

Contact details
Orpheus Island Resort, Private Mail Bag 15, Townsville Mail Centre QLD 4810. Tel: 1800 077 167. Email: admin@orpheus.com.au. Website: www.orpheus.com.au.

Silky Oaks Lodge

Where is it?
Silky Oaks Lodge is a wilderness retreat nestled on the edge of the Mossman Gorge in tropical North Queensland. Adjoining the World Heritage listed Daintree Rainforest National Park, the resort is seven km from the township of Mossman and 83 km north of Cairns.

Getting there
Silky Oaks Lodge is a five minute drive from the town of Mossman, 20 minutes north of Port Douglas and just over one hour north of Cairns. No public transport operates to the resort, so employees living outside of Mossman require their own car to get to work.

About the resort
Silky Oaks Lodge is an advanced accredited eco-tourism resort. Its ideal location on the Reef and near rainforests facilitates exploration of two World Heritage listed areas, the Great Barrier Reef and the Daintree Rainforest, and it is considered one of Australia's leading wilderness resorts. The resort is set on 28 acres and offers 60 stand alone chalets and the award winning Treehouse Restaurant. The resort also features a small conference facility.

To add to the guests' rainforest experience an array of nature based activities are available. Historical and cultural interpretive tours include Great Barrier Reef cruises, scenic flights, the Kuranda Skyrail and environmental guided safaris operated by Silky Oaks' own 4WD company, Australian Wilderness Experience. The lodge also has its own healing waters spa.

The lodge attracts 75 per cent of its business from international visitors with the majority coming from North America. The market mix includes well travelled couples and exclusive tour groups but does not cater for children under twelve years of age. The lodge has gained Eco Certification: Advanced Ecotourism meaning it has passed certain economic, ecological and social sustainability criteria as determined by Ecotourism Australia.

Peak season

Peak season is generally from July through to December. January is also busy with American and Europeans guests.

Working at Silky Oaks Lodge

Silky Oaks Lodge often has positions in most areas including front office, food and beverage, kitchen, housekeeping, activities, guest relations and administration.

Number of employees

There are approximately 75 to 85 team members working at Silky Oaks depending on the season. The majority of staff live off-site while a few staff members including the general manager and the assistant manager live at the resort.

Living arrangements

Most employees live in Port Douglas or Mossman or in other close by areas such as Newell Beach or Wonga Beach. Local real estate agents are available to assist you with accommodation.

Contact details

Visit the Voyages Hotels and Resorts website, where you will find an online employment application form to fill-in. Website: www.voyages.com.au/corporate/careers. Go to www.silkyoakslodge.com.au for information on the lodge itself.

New South Wales

Novotel Opal Cove Resort

Where is it?

Opal Cove Resort is on the north coast of NSW approximately 580 km north of Sydney. The resort is 200 m to a secluded beach, 10 minutes from the town centre of Coffs Harbour, 15 minutes from Coffs Harbour domestic airport and 10 minutes from a coach terminal and railway station.

Getting there

By plane to Coffs Harbour airport or by car, but buses also run up and down the Pacific Highway on a daily basis.

About the resort

Located in Korora Bay, Coffs Harbour, the resort is on absolute beachfront land and is perfect for families and conference delegates. The resort aims to attract both the business and family markets. The resort has a nine hole golf course, tennis courts, swimming pools, spas, gym and a kids club.

Working at Opal Cove

Work is available in the food and beverage area, housekeeping, front office duties, building maintenance, grounds maintenance, human resources, accounts, on-site retail stores and in organising recreational activities.

Number of employees

Depending on the time of year, the resort employs between 170 and 200 staff.

Living arrangements

There is no on-site accommodation for staff but there is reasonably priced accommodation in and around Coffs Harbour.

Contact details

Human Resources Department, Novotel Opal Cove Resort, Pacific Highway, Coffs Harbour NSW 2450. Tel: (02) 6651 0510. Website: www.accorhotels.com.au/corporate/job_opportunities.asp.

Tasmania

Cradle Mountain Lodge

Where is it?
Cradle Mountain Lodge is a wilderness retreat set on the northern edge of the World Heritage listed 131,920 ha Cradle Mountain/Lake St Clair National Park in north western Tasmania.

Getting there
Devonport and Burnie are the closest cities with airport and port facilities. The Spirit of Tasmania ferry crosses Bass Strait from Melbourne to Devonport two to three times per week. There are daily flights from Melbourne and Sydney to Devonport and Launceston airports.

Coach transfers are available from Devonport and Launceston airports, with only a limited service during spring and winter. Rental cars are available at Devonport and Launceston. It takes about three and a half hours to drive from Hobart.

About the lodge
The winner of numerous awards including state tourism awards for Best Resort and Environmental Tourism, Cradle Mountain Lodge is a world apart. A wilderness retreat with comfortable cabins, cosy log fires, companionable bars and fine food and wines. All cabins feature wood-burning fires and 28 of these cabins are complete with private spas and queen sized beds. The resort also offers conference facilities. Outside the wilderness beckons with a range of daily guided activities depending on the season. Walks, 4WD tours, abseiling, fly fishing, canoeing, mountain bike tours or horse riding are all on offer. Within the Lodge guests can relax with a massage or sauna or learn about Tasmanian wine and cheese.

The Lodge attracts couples and families but also has a strong group market in summer. It caters for conference groups mainly in the winter months. Approximately 80 per cent of the guests come from mainland Australia with the rest mostly from the UK, US and Germany.

Peak season

Peak season is the warmer months from October to April though there are visitors year round. Snow however, can and does fall on occasions during the summer.

Working at Cradle Mountain Lodge

The resort offers employment opportunities in food and beverage, housekeeping, front office duties, leisure activities and retail.

Number of employees

There are approximately 70 employees working at Cradle Mountain Lodge. Half of these live on site, with the remainder living in nearby towns.

Living at Cradle Mountain Lodge

The staff residential area is located approximately 200 m from the Lodge and is accessible by road or a short walk. There are four main staff accommodation blocks. Each block has an open plan communal area with a lounge with TV and video and a kitchen with full cooking facilities. A laundry with washing, drying and ironing facilities is also available. Each block contains an average of six to eight rooms.

Employees share a room during the summer months and during winter when staff numbers are lower single rooms are available. Each room is furnished and has electric heating. There are a number of A-frame houses with self contained cooking facilities for senior department heads.

Staff recreation facilities include the Bull Bar where the staff hold parties, BBQs, play pool or use the gym equipment. Latest release videos are also available for the staff to borrow free of charge. Employees are charged a nominal amount for accommodation, currently around $36 per week.

Contact details

Visit the Voyages, Hotels and Resorts website, where you will find an online employment application form to fill-in. Website: www.voyages.com.au/corporate/careers. Go to www.cradlemountainlodge.com.au for information on the lodge itself.

Western Australia

El Questro Wilderness Park

Where is it?

A 405,000 ha property, El Questro is located on the eastern perimeter of the Kimberley region, and extends for approximately 80 kilometres into the heart of the region. More specifically, it is located in the East Kimberley, 110 km west of Kununurra by road of which 58 km is on the sealed Great Northern Highway towards Wyndham and the remainder on the unsealed and corrugated gravel Gibb River Road.

About the wilderness park

El Questro Wilderness Park is without doubt, one of the world's unique holiday destinations. A working cattle station with a herd of approximately 5000 head of crossbred Brahman and Shorthorn cattle, El Questro was developed in 1991 to provide a truly outback Australian station holiday experience.

El Questro offers a diverse range of activities for the eco-tourist, agri-tourist and sports tourist alike. Whether it's photographing butterflies, fishing for barramundi or 4WD expeditions. El Questro is all about once-in-a-lifetime experiences.

Guests can experience boating through the Chamberlain Gorge or relaxing in the thermal pools of Zebedee Springs. Horse trekking is a fabulous way to observe all kinds of Kimberley wildlife. Accompanied by El Questro rangers, guests will be introduced to a wide variety of animals, birds and maybe even a saltwater crocodile.

Working at El Questro Wilderness Park

El Questro Wilderness Park has a smaller staff intake than many other resorts, but positions do come up in areas including food and beverage and cleaning.

Contact details

Visit the Voyages, Hotels and Resorts website, where you will find an online employment application form to fill-in. Website: www.voyages.com.au/corporate/careers.

Novotel Vines Resort

Where is it?
Located in Western Australia's oldest wine growing region, the Swan Valley, Novotel Vines Resort is 40 minutes drive north-east of Perth and 20 minutes from Perth Airport.

About the resort
Framed by the foothills of the Darling Ranges guests can choose to visit restaurants, wineries, art galleries and craft centres around the region.

The resort caters to both families and business conferences.

Working at Novotel Vines Resort
Typical resort work is available including food and beverage work, front of house duties, housekeeping and maintenance.

Number of employees
The resort employs 140 staff.

Living arrangements
No accommodation is provided on the resort. Nearby accommodation needs to be organised.

Contact details
Novotel Vines Resort, Verdelho Drive, The Vines WA 6069. Tel: (08) 9297 3000. Website: www.accorhotels.com.au/corporate/job_opportunities.asp.

Northern Territory

Voyages Hotels and Resorts: Ayers Rock, Kings Canyon and Alice Springs

Where are these resorts?
These resorts are run by Ayers Rock Resort Management. Ayers Rock Resort is located in the township of Yulara, adjacent to the Uluru-Kata Tjuta National Park, home of Uluru (Ayers Rock) and Kata Tjuta (Mt Olga), some 450 km south-west of Alice Springs.

Kings Canyon Resort and Alice Springs Resort, as the names indicate are found at Kings Canyon, which is half way between Yulara and Alice Springs, and in Alice Springs. Visitors can select between the comfort and hospitality of the Alice Springs Resort, the wilderness of Kings Canyon, or the luxury and wonder of Ayers Rock Resort.

Getting there

Yulara and Kings Canyon are serviced by bus from Alice Springs.

About the resorts

Ayers Rock Resort welcomes over 400,000 international and domestic visitors each year who go to experience the natural wonders of the central Australian region. To enhance the guests' experience, Ayers Rock Resort offers a variety of facilities ranging from a five-star hotel to camping grounds plus award-winning conference facilities. They also boast nine food and beverage outlets ranging from buffet to fine dining restaurants and the award winning Sounds of Silence restaurant under the stars. With all this they have plenty of reasons for needing qualified and experienced staff.

Kings Canyon Resort receives about 250,000 visitors each year and offers 96 standard hotel rooms, 32 deluxe spa rooms, 37 lodge rooms and a caravan and camping ground.

Alice Springs Resort has 108 standard rooms, 36 deluxe rooms, an award winning restaurant, lounge, pool bar and conference facilities for up to 150 people.

Working for Ayers Rock Resort

The management group offers a wide variety of employment options including assistant managers, food and beverage attendants, fine dining attendants, room attendants, housekeeping supervisors, chef de partie, demi chefs, commis chefs, hotel receptionists, reception supervisors, restaurant managers and shift leaders.

The isolation of the Ayers Rock and Kings Canyon resorts means additional staff are necessary to keep the resorts operational. Ayers Rock, for example, has its own power station, childcare centre, primary school, community library, medical centre and emergency services. At the time of writing it was advertising for a plumber and a refrigeration mechanic.

Number of employees

The group employs approximately 1200 staff.

Living at the resorts

Full board is provided to staff but a charge for accommodation is taken out of employees' salaries.

Contact details

Visit the Voyages, Hotels and Resorts website, where you will find an online employment application form to fill-in. Website:www.voyages.com.au/corporate/careers.

Casino work

Casinos in Australia offer work opportunities in the gaming rooms as well as in the attached resort or accommodation facilities that accompany most casinos. This section provides an overview of the many jobs available, as well as contact details for some of the larger casinos.

One of the great things about being trained for casino work is that this skill is something you can use during a working holiday. Although rules for certain games can vary slightly from country to country, your experience and good references will enable you to secure work during travels beyond Australia if you're planning to do this.

Working in a casino can offer more variety than just dealing on a gaming table. The turnover in casual casino staff should also allow you to pick up employment as you move from state to state. The pay is at award rates or above, which normally includes a number of penalty rates for such things as late shifts making this type of work an excellent option if you are thinking about settling down for a few of months to top up the piggy bank.

Additionally, if you have skills in serving beverages or dealing on high-roller tables, the tips from winners can be generous, and a friendly manner with the customers may bring in your own little fortune.

Employment opportunities

Casino division

Dealer

The role of the dealer is to deal the various games within the casino in a skilled and professional manner. To work in this position, it is essential that applicants undergo training at one of the in-house dealer training schools which run courses periodically throughout the year for suitable applicants.

178 Work around Australia

1 Conrad Treasury Casino - Brisbane
2 Conrad Jupiters Casino - Broadbeach
3 Star Casino - Sydney
4 Casino - Canberrra
5 Crown Casino - Melbourne
6 Wrestpoint Casino - Hobart
7 SKYCITY - Adelaide
8 Burswood Casino - Perth
9 SKYCITY - Darwin

Keno writer

Keno writers are responsible for validating Keno tickets for patrons, paying out prize winners, assisting with the running of the games, and answering any queries that guests may have regarding Keno. Cash handling experience, together with excellent customer service skills, are essential.

Video attendant

The role of a video attendant is to provide assistance to guests regarding the types of video games available, as well as assist with guest payouts and any other queries regarding the functioning of the machines.

Security

Security officers are responsible for maintaining required standards of dress and behaviour among guests and ensuring that guests, staff and the casino is protected from any immoral and/ or illegal activities. A police clearance is required as part of the application process.

Surveillance

The surveillance department's primary responsibility is to provide adequate protection, security and surveillance of the casino's facilities and operations, its patrons and its employees, using a sophisticated closed circuit television (CCTV) system and security alarm system. Previous experience in a casino environment is an advantage, and experience in surveillance is desirable. As with security positions, a police clearance usually needs to be submitted with your application.

Food and beverage division

Busperson

This role is to assist in the food outlets. It involves clearing tables, maintaining stock within the restaurants and providing guests with professional and efficient service.

Bar useful

The main duties of a bar useful include clearing empty glasses in the bar and surrounding areas, helping the bar attendants set up the bar, and assisting with running the bar. This position is generally seen as the stepping stone to becoming a bar attendant.

Drink steward

Drink stewards are responsible for serving drinks to guests playing at the tables or relaxing in the bars. Basic beer, wine and cocktail knowledge is advantageous.

Bar attendant

People wishing to gain employment as a bar attendant would normally have either a minimum of 12 months previous cocktail experience or experience in the position of bar useful or drink steward.

Wait staff

Applicants for positions as wait staff must have a vibrant personality and good presentation to ensure that they cater to their guests' needs. Previous experience is preferred but may not be essential in some outlets.

Kitchen staff

Operating large commercial kitchens requires a workforce of kitchen hands, stewards, cooks and chefs.

Rooms division

Concierge

First impressions at any of the large casino resorts is extremely important, and the concierge department is the first to meet and greet the hotel guests. The porters are responsible for helping guests with luggage, explaining room and resort facilities and valet car parking. The concierge desk helps guests with general enquiries about the resort, as well as booking tours and organising car hire. Applicants will require a clean driving record, excellent interpersonal skills, physical fitness and a good knowledge of the local area.

Front office staff

This department is responsible for attending to accommodation enquiries and bookings, guest check-in/check-out and finalisation of guest accounts. People wishing to gain employment as a front office clerk require a pleasant outgoing personality, strong customer service skills, understanding of different cultures, keyboard skills and excellent presentation.

Communications

The communications department consists of an extremely busy switchboard that handles a large volume of calls each day. Previous experience on a busy switchboard is normally required.

Recreation officers

The recreation centres at casino resorts normally consist of a fully equipped gymnasium, fitness classes, heated indoor pool, spa, sauna and possibly tennis courts. To work as a recreation co-ordinator, applicants require a tertiary qualification in a relevant field, a current first aid certificate and in some cases, a lifesaver bronze medallion. Other positions include recreation attendants and nannies.

Housekeepers

The housekeeping department is responsible for creating a home away from home for guests by providing clean rooms and facilities. Positions include room attendants and house porters, with previous experience in a similar position desirable.

Queensland

Conrad Treasury Casino - Brisbane

Located in a grand heritage setting, right in the heart of Brisbane, the Conrad Treasury Casino offers a world of first class entertainment, 24 hours a day. It is promoted as offering the best of both worlds—a deluxe hotel and the excitement of a world class casino. Conrad Treasury Casino is situated at the top of the Queen Street Mall in the centre of Brisbane, approximately 20 minutes drive from the domestic and international airports. Undercover parking for 750 vehicles is available on-site and it can also be easily reached by public transport.

Applying for a position

Send applications to: Human Resources Department, Conrad Treasury, PO Box 2488, Brisbane QLD 4001. Tel: 1800 506 888. Email: treashr@conrad.com.au. Website: www.conrad.com.au.

Conrad Jupiters Casino – Broadbeach

Conrad Jupiters was opened in 1985 and is situated on Broadbeach Island, in the heart of Queensland's famous Gold Coast, a 20 minute drive from Coolangatta Airport or one hour from Brisbane Airport. Coach services, limousines and buses provide transfers from Coolangatta and Brisbane airports. A private shuttle service is also available from Brisbane Airport. The casino has over 1000 gaming machines and about 100 table games. Details on other facilities can be found on their website below.

Applying for a position

Send applications to: The Recruitment Centre, Conrad Jupiters Casino, PO Box 1515, Broadbeach QLD 4218. Tel: 1800 074 144. Tel: (07) 5592 1133. Email: cjhrd@ conrad.com.au. Website: www.jupiters.com.au.

New South Wales

Star City Casino – Sydney

The Victorian based TABCORP, one of Australia's largest entertainment and leisure companies, owns and operates Star City Casino, the only casino in New South Wales. It is located on Sydney Harbour and opened for business in September 1995, but it was not until late 1997 that the permanent casino and hotel complex was completed.

The casino has 200 gaming tables and 1500 gaming machines catering to a diverse range of customers. In addition to the casino, Star City includes a 500 room hotel and apartment complex, two theatres each with a seating capacity of over 1000, seven major restaurants and a nightclub. It also operates a large banquet and convention facility.

Applying for a position

Send applications to: Star City Casino, 80 Pyrmont Street, Pyrmont NSW 2009. Tel: Recruitment Hotline (02) 9657 8887. Website: www.starcity.com.au.

Australian Capital Territory

Casino Canberra

Casino Canberra is located in Glebe Park, Canberra and is situated among 20 ha of parks and gardens. The complex includes Casino Canberra, Parkroyal Hotel, the National Convention Centre and the Royal Theatre. The Casino is adjacent to Canberra's CBD.

There are several bars and restaurants, live entertainment on Friday and Saturday nights and numerous tables playing all games.

Applying for a position

Send applications to: Human Resources, Casino Canberra, Glebe Park, 21 Binara Street, Canberra City ACT 2601. Website: www.casinocanberra.com.au.

Victoria

Crown Casino - Melbourne

Crown Casino, promoted as 'the world of entertainment', provides employment for more than 8000 people. To be considered for work with Crown Casino applicants must be 18 years of age or older and have Australian citizenship, permanent residency in Australia or an appropriate work visa. With 40 restaurants and food outlets, 30 bars, 300 tables and live entertainment there is plenty of work.

Applying for a position

You will need to complete an application form and forward your application to: Crown Human Resources, 8 Whiteman Street, Southbank VIC 3006. Tel: Crown Recruitment (03) 9292 7777. You can also apply online at www.crownjobs.com.au.

Tasmania

Wrestpoint Casino - Hobart

Wrestpoint Casino was Australia's first casino, having opened in February 1973. Although small compared to the more recent entertainment and gaming venues, it caters for players of all standards and wallet sizes. There are over 490 machines in the 278 room hotel.

Applying for a position

Send applications to: Wrestpoint Casino, 410 Sandy Bay Road, Sandy Bay TAS 7005. Tel: (03) 6221 1780. Email: employment@wrestpoint.com.au. Website: www.wrestpoint.com.au.

South Australia

SKYCITY - Adelaide

Renamed in 2001 after Adelaide Casino was purchased by SKYCITY Entertainment Group the casino is located in Adelaide's historic railway station. This non-stop casino has 90 gaming tables, 950 gaming machines, eight restaurants and bars along with live entertainment. It is the tenth largest employer in Adelaide.

Applying for a position

Send applications to Human Resources, SKYCITY Adelaide, GPO Box 1918, Adelaide SA 5001 or fill out the application on the website. Tel: (08) 8218 4182. Email: employment@skycityadelaide.com.au. Website: www.skycityadelaide.com.au.

Western Australia

Burswood Casino Resort - Perth

Burswood Casino Resort has a 24-hour casino, nine restaurants and five bars, Perth's leading international five-star hotel, the 413 room Burswood Hotel, a multifunctional Convention Centre, non-stop live entertainment in the Casino Cabaret Lounge, the Burswood Theatre and the largest indoor stadium in Australia, the Burswood Dome.

Applying for a position

Applications can be obtained from the Human Resources Department and completed forms should be sent to: The Human Resources Department, Burswood International Resort Casino, PO Box 500, Victoria Park WA 6979. Tel: (08) 9362 7524. Email: recruit@burswood.com.au. Website: www.burswood.com.au.

Northern Territory

SKYCITY - Darwin

Located close to Mindil Beach, Darwin's casino complex includes 117 hotel rooms, four restaurants, five bars, leisure and conference facilities along with gaming tables and over 500 slot machines.

Applying for a position

Send your application to Recruitment, SKYCITY – Darwin, GPO Box 3846, Darwin NT 0801. Tel: (08) 8943 8888. Email: careers@skycitydarwin.com.au. Web: www.skycitydarwin.com.au. There is a section on the website for working holiday makers who are interested in working for SKYCITY while they are in Darwin.

1 Perisher Blue
2 Thredbo
3 Mt Buller
4 Falls Creek

Ski fields work

So, you're thinking about spending three to four months working in a ski resort? Well your dream is shared by thousands of others every year, but if you have the motivation, coupled with some experience, why not pursue your idea? It's certainly a different lifestyle for most, and although you'll probably spend every cent you earn on food, beer and a bed, you'll leave the melting slopes at the end of spring with memories to last a lifetime!

Australia's four largest ski season employers are detailed below. Apart from jobs out on the snow, there is quite a large variety of work in hospitality as well as other work that sometimes goes unnoticed, such as garbage collection and housekeeping.

If you love skiing, take note of the many staff benefits that are associated with working for one of the big four ski resorts.

First, a word of warning! Because of the relatively low altitude of Australian mountains and the strength of the Australian sun, even in winter, snow conditions can vary from day to day. Although resorts attempt to bridge the gap between what Mother Nature drops from the sky and what is required to keep customers happy on the slopes with snow making machinery, your employment is subject to both snow and weather conditions.

Perisher Blue

Where is it?

Perisher Blue is one of the two main ski resorts in NSW serviced by the town of Jindabyne. It is located in the Snowy Mountains approximately 450 km south-west of Sydney.

Getting there

By car

Jindabyne is an easy two hour drive from Canberra, and a five to six hour drive from Sydney via Canberra and Cooma, with over half the journey on dual carriageway roads. It is around seven hours from Melbourne by road.

By air

Qantas flies from Sydney or Melbourne to the Snowy Mountains Airport which is 50 km, or around 45 minutes drive, from Jindabyne. Alternatively, you can fly to Canberra airport with Qantas, and then drive a comfortable two hours to Jindabyne. Taxi transfers and car rental facilities are available from both airports. The Snow Express shuttle meets all flights to and from the Snowy Mountains Airport but seat bookings on 1800 679 754 are essential. The Snow Express operates year round.

By bus

Greyhound Australia operates a service between Canberra and Jindabyne. For information regarding services and prices call 13 20 30.

About the resort

Perisher Blue operates the largest ski resort in the Southern Hemisphere. It is located within the Kosciuszko National Park in the beautiful Snowy Mountains region of southern NSW. Perisher Blue boasts four ski areas, 1250 ha of ski terrain, 50 lifts and the capacity to lift 47,600 snow sliders per hour. The company also operates the Perisher Valley Hotel, a four and a half star boutique 'on snow' hotel, the Station Resort Hotel, located five km from Jindabyne, and the Skitube underground railway which transports several hundred thousand passengers each season from below the snow line to the Perisher Blue and Blue Cow ski areas.

Type of work

Ski Area

The Ski Area is the largest department in the resort and is responsible for everything from the lower slopes to the highest peaks. Lift operators are the face of the resort and maintain the ramps, mazes, and loading and unloading areas while ensuring guest safety on the chairlift system. Ski patrollers are trained for all medical emergencies, to respond to injuries on the mountain and to police dangerous skiing and snowboarding. Groomer drivers maintain and groom all runs throughout the resort, while snowmakers work through the night to create the best quality surface of snow. Transport drivers are responsible for operating shuttle buses, distributing goods delivered to the resort and assisting car park attendants with traffic control, security and greeting guests who choose to drive to the resort. Trail crew are involved in a variety of roles from helping prepare for on-mountain events to ensuring all building surrounds are clear of snow and ice. Lift fitters, mechanics and electricians are responsible for the regular servicing and emergency repairs of all Perisher Blue lifts, vehicles, machinery and property.

Concourse

Concourse attendants work at the three Skitube buildings and assist guests with platform safety, crowd control, ticket auditing, luggage handling and information about the resort.

Ski and Snowboard School

With over 300 qualified professionals employed each season, the Ski and Snowboard School runs a Hiring Clinic for everyone interested in becoming a Perisher Blue instructor. If you are certified and have experience instructing in Australia, the Ski and Snowboard School also employs qualified child-care assistants, crèche attendants and ticket sellers.

Guest Services

Mountain hosts ensure a great guest experience by providing information about the resort and services available as well as taking guests on guided tours across the mountains.

Perisher Blue Snow Holidays

Reservation consultants assist guests with accommodation information and bookings from their office in Jindabyne.

Hotels, Food and Beverage Department

The Perisher Valley Hotel has 31 rooms, a cocktail bar, nightclub and a fine dining restaurant. The Station Resort Hotel sleeps 1500 guests in 254 rooms, and includes a food court, char grill and pizza station, nightclub and bars. The Food and Beverage Department is based at Blue Cow Mountain and services food and beverage outlets throughout the resort. Positions available include cocktail and bar attendants, cellar attendants, butchers, bakers, chefs a la carte, breakfast chefs, chefs for Mexican, Italian and Asian styles, preparation and short order cooks, kitchen hands, disc jockeys, food servers, table attendants, cashiers, front office receptionists and reservation officers, night auditors, porters, head housekeepers, room attendants, night cleaners, laundry attendants and stores people.

Ticket sellers

Ticket sellers are the front line customer service staff, who assist guests to find the ticket package that best suits their needs.

Skitube staff

Train drivers are responsible for transporting passengers on the underground railway from Bullock's Flat (outside Jindabyne) to Perisher Valley and Blue Cow Mountain.

Accommodation and benefits for staff

Clean, warm and reasonably priced accommodation is available on the mountain, at the Station Resort and in the township of Jindabyne.

Staff benefits include:

- a staff season pass (retail value $1200); an administration fee applies
- free skiing at Perisher, Smiggins, Blue Cow and Guthega
- subsidised staff accommodation
- free ski/snowboard lessons
- a 20 per cent discount in food and retail outlets
- discounted ski/snowboard hire
- employee recognition program
- uniforms for all guest contact and outdoor staff

- season passes for dependants after completion of five consecutive seasons of service
- long service awards after 10, 20 and 30 years of service.

Contact details

Written applications should be stapled in the top left hand corner (don't send your application in a folder). Your covering letter should clearly state your first two choices of position in order of preference. Your resume should include references (copies only). Allow an additional day for mail to reach Perisher Valley.

Mail your resume marked 'Winter Application' to: Human Resources Manager, Perisher Blue Pty Limited, PO Box 42, Perisher Valley NSW 2624. You can also apply online at: www.perisherblue.com.au.

All employment offers are subject to favourable snow and weather conditions. The season begins mid June and ends mid October. There is no guarantee of employment for the entire winter season.

Thredbo

Where is it?

Thredbo is situated on the Alpine Way 33 km south of Jindabyne in the Snowy Mountains of NSW.

About the resort

Thredbo boasts the longest vertical ski drop in Australia at 672 m and the longest run at five and a half kilometres. The resort is in the valley and this can mean that the village is wet and slushy though the snow higher up may be quite good. The chairlifts run up out from the village. The village has a European feel including an after-dark apré-ski fun atmosphere.

Getting there

Thredbo is an easy five to six hour drive from Sydney and seven hours from Melbourne via the scenic Kosciuszko Alpine Way.

The nearest commercial airport is at Cooma, 85 km from Thredbo, where transfers or car hire are available. Qantas flies from Sydney. Alternatively, Greyhound Australia operates a daily bus service to Thredbo from Sydney, Melbourne and Brisbane via Canberra.

Working at Thredbo

General positions

Reservations sales agents are needed from mid March until the end of August. Call centre staff are required for booking accommodation on the computer reservations system for Thredbo Village. Previous travel agent, reservations or sales experience is required, and applicants must be enthusiastic, friendly and service orientated.

Ticket sellers are front-line customer service staff who are required to sell lift and ski school tickets. This work involves accurately balancing all transactions including cash and credit cards. Previous cash handling experience is an advantage. The position requires excellent customer service skills.

Lift attendants assist customers on and off ski lifts in a safe manner, run T-bars and assist customers on chairlifts. An ability to ski/snowboard is an advantage. There is a minimum age of 21 years for applicants. Ticket checkers check lift tickets and ID passes of all customers and staff, control lift queues and undertake general duties.

Snow groomers groom and maintain all ski runs and T-bar tracks, and drive grooming machines. Previous experience is desirable and a mechanical knowledge is an advantage. A truck licence is required.

Ski patrollers provide immediate first aid to injured skiers, erect and maintain safety equipment and carry out speed control and slope duties. Applicants must hold an advanced level first aid certificate (minimum requirement) and be able to handle an akja. Previous patrol experience is essential. Minimum age 21 years.

Rental staff fit and issue ski hire equipment and rental clothing to customers. Staff are responsible for accurate and legible completion of rental forms and maintenance of equipment. Prior sales and cash handling experience is an advantage. Technical sales staff must have knowledge of and an ability to sell skis, ski boots, snowboards and boots.

Ski repair technicians must be specialised in all areas of ski and snowboard repair. Previous experience in the use of Montana equipment is an advantage.

Garbage collectors are needed for the resort. Applicants should be enthusiastic people willing to work outdoors during the day collecting refuse and recycling products from all areas of the village, and assisting with compacting the refuse. Attention to occupational health and safety issues is essential as is a current drivers licence.

Bus drivers are needed to drive 45 seat Leyland buses for a shuttle service and 20 seat Toyota Coaster buses around the village to pick up guests. A class MR licence is required and previous experience is an advantage. A friendly and outgoing nature is essential.

Hotel positions

Room attendants are required for cleaning and restocking of hotel rooms and apartments. A friendly and courteous disposition is required. Cleaners are required to clean and maintain hotel public areas, restaurants and bars. Some heavy lifting is required. Night and day shifts are available. Applicants must be friendly, reliable and courteous and hold a current drivers licence.

Reservations sales agents are needed to operate the computer accommodation bookings for Thredbo Village. Previous travel agent, reservations or sales experience is required. Applicants must be enthusiastic, friendly and service orientated.

Reception and reservation staff greet hotel guests on arrival, and check-in and check-out guests from their hotel or apartment using the Fidelio computer system. Previous hotel front office and cash handling experience is essential.

Demi chefs and commis chefs are required to cook in the bistro and a la carte restaurants. Health and safety awareness is essential. Kitchen hands are needed to assist in the resort kitchens, including cleaning, washing up and storing orders. Some heavy work is involved. Health and safety awareness is essential.

Food and beverage staff are needed including waiting and bar staff to assist in a la carte or bistro services and/or one of the five bars operated by the hotel. Keen, well presented, enthusiastic people with previous experience and references are sought and an RSA Certificate is required. Cellar and stores staff to carry out food stock rotation and issuing to various outlets. Previous experience in beer reticulation and stock handling is essential. Some heavy lifting may be required.

Ski/Snowboard instructors

Generally a person must be a class three or higher standard skier/snowboarder. Apart from technical experience, instructors are required to be well groomed, polite, friendly, able to communicate in a confident and enthusiastic manner, and willing to improve their skills.

Each ski resort has an Instructors Clinic at the beginning of the season, usually in June. Therefore, a person interested in instructing must choose the resort at which he or she wishes to work and attend that resort's Instructors Clinic. Contact Thredbo about their Instructors Clinic by email at: recruitment@thredbo.com.au. Leave plenty of time to make arrangements.

Accommodation for staff

Housing can be provided in Jindabyne, the service town for the ski resorts. Apartments are fully furnished and self-contained with kitchens and laundry facilities.

Contact details

Contact the address below and request an application. Post applications to: Kosciuszko Thredbo Personnel Department, PO Box 92, Thredbo Alpine Village NSW 2625. Enquiries can be emailed to: recruitment@thredbo.com.au. Website: www.thredbo.com.au.

Mt Buller

Where is it?

Mt Buller is located in the Victorian Alps north-east of Melbourne via Yarra Glen, Yea and Mansfield.

Getting there

It is a three and a half hour drive from Melbourne with coaches departing daily from Melbourne.

About the resort

The resort offers 26 lifts for downhill skiing with runs for beginners up to expert level. The village is above the snowline and offers a range of restaurants and activities to see visitors through 'white out' days.

Type of work

Opportunities exist for bar staff, housekeepers, ski technicians, table clearers, kitchen hands, snow groomers, cashiers, lift attendants, snow makers, chefs, porters, ticket sellers, child-care workers, receptionists, waiters, cooks, retail sales staff, assistant front office staff, ski and snowboarding instructors.

Accommodation and benefits for staff

Full-time employees may be eligible for subsidised staff housing. All accommodation is shared with two to four other workers. Some lodges offer full board, with others providing cooking facilities. The cost of rent varies according to the type of housing, with bed only charged at $60 to $100 per week and full board costing $155 per week.

Staff who are employed full-time for the season, even if employed on casual rates, receive complimentary ski lift season passes. In addition, returning staff who have worked full-time the season before receive five complimentary half-price day tickets. Those who worked full-time for the previous two seasons receive complimentary ski lift season passes for their spouse or bona fide de facto and dependant children, or ten half price day tickets. Seasonal staff are also eligible for a 20 per cent discount at all food and beverage outlets, discounts at the Lifesavers Tubing Park and Ski School lessons.

Staff who are normally employed for less than 38 hours per week receive a complimentary ski lift pass only when required to carry out assigned duties for the purpose of access.

Conditions of work

Employees are expected to work a five-day week with the opportunity for additional hours, however this is subject to snow conditions. Staff are paid weekly via direct deposit into a bank account. Rates of pay vary in accordance with qualifications and experience.

It is strongly advised that all employees have a current ambulance subscription and it is mandatory for all overseas employees to have their own travel insurance.

Contact details

For more information concerning employment at Mt Buller contact: Buller Ski Lifts, PO Box 1, Mt Buller VIC 3723. Tel: (03) 5777 6052. Website: www.mtbuller.com.au.

Falls Creek

Where is it?

Falls Creek is in Victoria approximately four and a half hours drive from Melbourne via the Hume Highway. Take the turn off at the Milawa sign post and proceed to Mount Beauty. Falls Creek is about another 30 kms from Mount Beauty and found on the boundary of the Bogong High Plains.

Getting there

Found in the Victorian Alps it is easily reached from both Melbourne and Albury. Coaches run daily from Melbourne and Albury.

About the resort

With over 450 ha of fantastic ski terrain Falls Creek is Victoria's largest ski resort. These natural resources are combined with the largest snow making system in Victoria. The friendly village is located above the snowline with spectacular views of the Bogong and Spion Kopje mountains and the Rocky Valley Dam. A helicopter service links Mt Hotham and Falls Creek resorts.

Working at Falls Creek

Falls Creek Ski Lifts operates:
- the ski lifts

- the Snowsport School
- ticket sales
- the snow making system
- the grooming department
- Cloud 9 Restaurant
- Frying Pan Inn Hotel
- Dicky Knees Cafe
- the Falls Creek Reservation Centre.

Staff are recruited for the operations listed above. All other businesses within the resort recruit their own staff and need to be contacted directly.

Accommodation for staff

Discounted on-mountain shared accommodation is available, but some staff stay off the mountain in the township of Mt Beauty.

Contact details

All details can be found on the website: www.fallscreek.com.au.

198 Work around Australia

1 Townsville
2 Bowen
3 Mackay
4 Rockhampton
5 Gladstone
6 Port Hedland
7 Karratha
8 Newman

Mining work

Growth of the mining industry

Though it was once true that 'Australia rides on the sheep's back' because wool was such a large percentage of Australian exports, these days Australia's export mix is more diversified. The mining industry has always being significant, making up about 35 per cent of Australia's exports in value. As the world's largest exporter of coal, iron ore, lead, diamonds, rutile, zinc and zinconium and the second largest exporter of gold and uranium, Australia ships a lot of rock.

However, a new and largely unexpected (certainly unplanned) development has been the rapid growth in demand from China in particular, for a wide range of minerals along with gas. Driven by incessant growth in China the mining industry is scrambling to build the infrastructure and labour force necessary to meet the demands of this new and hungry customer.

All states are benefiting to some extent but it is Western Australia and Queensland where growth is surging. In 2006 Western Australia's output of commodities jumped 29 per cent to a huge $43.2 billion mostly from oil, gas and iron ore. This works out at about $5 million per hour of shipments to export markets. There are currently 24 major mineral and energy projects under way in the state to be completed by the end of 2007 which are worth $5.8 billion. These projects will facilitate the ongoing boom that began about four years ago. Queensland is also sharing in the mining boom but focused more on coal where new projects are being developed as rapidly as possible.

Although it is estimated that some 320,000 people are directly and indirectly employed in the minerals and other extractive industries, a recent report suggests that the mineral industry will require an additional 70,000 workers by 2015 if it is to continue with its current growth. This is approximately a 76 per cent growth over the next 10 years with the greatest demand being for tradespeople

(27,000) and semiskilled workers who mostly operate equipment (22,000). In addition there will also be continued demand for professionals and unskilled workers. The report, released by the Minerals Council expects an extra 42,000 workers will be required for Western Australia, 15,000 in Queensland and about 5000 each in NSW and South Australia. There is no general agreement as to how long the boom will last but many analysts predict that the boom has some years yet to run before demand begins to slow.

Type of work

Many of the mining operations and developments in Australia are located in regional and often remote areas of Australia and this means it is more difficult to recruit and retain workers. Positions are found across the whole gamut of activities operated by mining companies and by the contracting service providers including exploration, mining, processing, transport, environmental management, community relations and administration. Within each of these areas the demand for labour ranges from professionals, managers, technicians, tradespeople to semiskilled and unskilled positions.

Not only is there a high demand for labour in the mining industry itself but also in the supporting services and infrastructure that allows the mines to operate. People are leaving local retail outlets and other businesses to work in the mines where the pay cannot be matched. There are reports of 19-year-olds in mines near Mackay earning $100,000 a year while truck drivers, labours and kitchen staff earn similar amounts in the Pilbara; even the earnings of cleaners is not far behind. The website of recruitment agency Hays confirms that the earnings in the main boom towns of Western Australia and Queensland for mine personnel start at about $80,000 regardless of the job. See www.hays.com.au/salay.

The hotspots

Although mining can be found throughout Australia much of it is mature and fully accounted for in the regional economy or is expanding slowly without a rapid demand for resources. Such is not the case with the boom states of Western Australia and Queensland. But even here, the real hotspots are the Pilbara, and in Queensland, the region centred on the Bowen Basin (a geological description where a vast amount of coal is located) that runs from behind Bowen in the north to south west of Gladstone around 500 km to the south. Some 85 per cent of the Queensland's coal comes from this area.

In 2006 $29 billion of the $43 billion earned from mining and energy in Western Australia came out of the Pilbara, a remote region, 1600 kms north of Perth. The reason Pilbara is such a hot spot is that both iron ore and offshore gas production are booming at the same time. Around 40,000 people live in this huge region with the largest towns being Port Hedland (13,000), Karratha (10,000) and Newman (4000). Much of the new development in support of the mines is focused on Karratha which has the largest shopping centre in the region but many negatives, like scarce and expensive housing. Very basic houses start at around $700 per week however, not everyone lives permanently in the region with many workers on fly in/fly out contracts. The boom shows in Karratha in many ways such as the town reputedly having more boats per head of population than any other area of Australia. The wages paid in the mines have filtered back to town with the manager of the local fast food chicken outlet earning some $2000 a week plus housing.

At the other side of the country, Mackay (82,000) in Queensland is another example of a town in the middle of a mining boom. Mackay is the centre of the largest sugar cane growing region in Australia, but farmers are struggling to find people to work in the fields as the mines pay much better. Mine workers are being paid around $100,000 depending on the level of qualifications and experience and even the professionals in Mackay like accountants are quitting to work in the mines. In order to continue as a going concern, Mackay's businesses are recruiting from overseas with the abattoir just having recruited 100 workers from Brazil while the pharmacies are recruiting from South Africa. As more locals are recruited into the mines, more positions in other occupational areas are opening up for those from further afield who are not able to work in the mines. Other nearby towns feeling the benefits of the mining boom are Bowen (9000) and Gladstone (28,000) where coal export ports are located (along with Mackay), Townsville (160,000) and Rockhampton (60,000). To quote one local in Mackay 'Business is booming but has been hamstrung because it can't find labour—whether it is financial advisors or plumbers.'

Finding a way in

This book is principally about short-term work in regional Australia and while the mining industry would be keener to employ full-time permanent employees (on contract) that is not always an option at present. It is almost a case of employing who turns up, to quote the rail manager at Pilbara Iron, 'If you have two arms, two legs and your heart is beating there's a job here ...' In addition, there are many jobs available in the towns servicing the mining operations, not necessarily at the same pay scales as in the mines, but much better than equivalent work in other parts of the country and a more likely source of short-term jobs.

Recruitment can be either directly with the mining company, through specialist recruitment agencies or more general agencies. Alternatively cold call when you are there. In general the recruitment hierarchy is that senior management and high level professionals with plenty of experience are recruited directly by the companies or specialists agencies while those with fewer skills and/or experience are more likely to be recruited by general agencies or by simply rolling up a the 'front door'. The higher up the employment ladder, the longer the time commitment required.

There are a number of useful websites (that mostly have links to job sites) providing a range of information about the industry. The website of the Australasian Institute of Mining and Metallurgy is a good portal with links to many other organisations in Australia and elsewhere for a wealth of information on mining. See www.ausimm.com.au. The website www.miningreference.com is a wide ranging portal to the mining industry that includes a jobs area for mostly professional and technical occupations but some other areas such as administration are also included along with links to recruiters.

There is a range of recruitment agencies for the mining industry broken, as usual, into the general employment agencies and the specialists. The web-based generalists which include vacancies from many different industries and sectors include: www.seek.com.au, www.careerone.com.au and www.mycareer.com.au. Also have a look at //employment.byron.com.au/jobs/jobs-in-wa-northern.html and //employment.byron.com.au/jobs/jobs-in-qld-central-coast.html.

The specialists include the following agencies as examples only; there are many more. There are many agencies based in Perth though increasingly both mining companies and these agencies are taking their message to the east coast of Australia.

www.miningemployment.com.au - with a focus on Western Australia but also with positions around Australia.

www.extremeworkforce.com.au - based in MacKay this recruitment agency recruits for the coal industry for wide range of positions in addition to other industries.

www.gsfaustralia.com - this is a recruitment agency for mobile plant operators.

www.constructive.net.au - this agency covers mining, infrastructure, building, oil and gas.

www.dtworkforce.com - specialises in contract and permanent para-professionals, tradespeople and unskilled personnel for mining, oil and gas and construction industries.

www.ansearch.com.au - a portal that will lead to other online agencies specialising in the mining industry.

The websites of the major mining and oil companies operating in the Pilbara include:

BHP Billiton - //jobs.bhpbilliton.com

Rio Tinto - www.pilbarairon.com.au

Fortescue Metals - www.fmgl.com.au

Woodside Petroleum - www.woodsidehiringnow.com.au

The websites of the 14 major coal companies operating in Queensland can be found on the Department of Natural Resources and Water's website at www.nrw.qld.gov.au/mines/coal/contacts.html. Each of these has employment information.

Much of the development of mines is subcontracted out as indicated by the Fortescue Metals website above. There are many contractors in this industry and a starting point (other than employment agencies) is the list of consultants and contractors found at www.miningreference.com.

More general employment agencies serving the towns can be found by going to //employment.byron.com.au/recruiters and searching by state. Scroll through the list to find the town that the agency is located in (though not all agencies are listed). In the Pilbara check out www.anyjob.org.au/pilbara.php for positions outside of the mining operations.

For working holiday makers

While residents and citizens can apply for vacancies without restriction, working holiday makers are limited by the the three-month rule. This prevents working holiday makers working for one employer for more than three months in a row. The other difficulty is that many of these positions in the mines are long term and some will require an induction or training period that would eat into the three-month period. However, semi-skilled and unskilled positions are more likely to be available for a three-month period, especially if you arrive 'on the scene'. In addition and a much more likely possibility, are the many businesses and services in the towns that are desperate for workers to replace those who have gone to work in the mines and to cope with the rapidly growing population. A major problem however, is often not gaining a job but finding somewhere to stay, especially in more isolated areas.

Working in the cities

This chapter offers you a head start to knowing where to find work in Australian cities. Many travellers fall into the trap of waiting until they arrive in a city before putting their minds to finding employment. If you use this book as a guide, you will certainly have an opportunity to dive straight into job hunting well before reaching your destination.

Employers are increasingly preferring contract, part-time and casual employees over full-time employees which is great if that is what you want. Temporary workers don't receive the benefits of permanent staff, however, the hourly rate is often higher which is great news for the traveller. An employer generally adopts a policy of taking on temporary staff to align their company's output with consumer demand for their products or services. This particularly occurs when staff workloads are inconsistent due to seasonal influences. More and more employers are finding the option of employing temporary staff attractive and there is certainly a growth in the number of employment agencies catering for this sector of the employment market.

The internet

Without a doubt, the best way to locate employment in the cities these days is though the internet. The foremost jobs website in Australia is SEEK, which can be found at www.seek.com.au. You can search based on type of job, location and whether you are looking for short-term or permanent positions. Also check out www.careerone.com.au and www.mycareer.com.au.

Alternatively, get hold of a copy of *Netting a Job in Australia and New Zealand*, also published by Global Exchange, which lists over 400 employment websites including those of use for the working traveller. More information on this book can be obtained by going to Global Exchange's website at www.globalexchange.com.au.

Newspapers

Major Australian newspapers are a wealth of information and for the resourceful jobseeker, a newspaper may be the first and last place you'll need to look for your first job.

From the point of view of understanding the work environment in Australia, newspapers can be a useful guide to gauge the relative remuneration for various positions, as well as the minimum requirements for a job. For example, if you intend taking temporary work in office administration, then the advertisements you see will give you a better understanding of pay rates, the availability of work and the minimum typing speed required to successfully secure a position.

Each major city in Australia has at least one daily newspaper, and the size of the employment section depends on the day. Below is a list of the major newspapers that have the best employment sections and recruitment advertising. The greatest number of jobs are advertised on Saturdays with a fewer number advertised on Wednesdays. One exception is *The Australian* which, in addition to Saturday advertising, advertises IT positions every Tuesday.

National newspapers

There are two national newspapers, *The Australian* found on the web at www.theaustralian.com.au and the *Australian Financial Review* at www.afr.com.au.

There are two rural weekly newspapers both published on Wednesday, *Stock & Land* at www.sl.farmonline.com.au and *The Weekly Times* at www.theweeklytimes.com.au.

Queensland

The *Courier Mail* is the main daily newspaper in Queensland at www.news.com.au/couriermail.

New South Wales

The *Sydney Morning Herald* is one of two state-wide daily newspapers at www.smh.com.au, the other is the *Daily Telegraph* at www.news.com.au/dailytelegraph.

ACT

The *Canberra Times* is the main daily newspaper in the ACT at //canberra.yourguide.com.au.

Victoria

The main state-wide newspapers in Victoria are *The Age* at www.theage.com.au and the *Herald Sun* at www.news.com.au/heraldsun.

Tasmania

The main state-wide newspapers in Tasmania are the *Mercury* at www.news.com.au/mercury and the *Examiner* at www.examiner.com.au.

South Australia

The main daily newspaper in South Australia is the *Adelaide Advertiser* at www.news.com.au/adelaidenow.

Western Australia

The *West Australian* is the main daily newspaper in Western Australia at //thewest.com.au.

Northern Territory

Northern Territory News is the main daily newspaper in the Territory at //newsmedianet.com.au.

Other newspapers and magazines

Regional cities such as Toowoomba, Newcastle, Dubbo, Sale or Albany have their own newspapers which may be useful for finding work in the local region. In the smaller towns often newspapers will be weeklies. Many recruitment agencies seeking working travellers for short-term and casual work regularly advertise in the giveaway newspapers and magazines aimed at backpackers. These can be found in the major cities where backpackers congregate. *TNT Magazine* at www.tntmagazine.com.au is the best example.

University and college noticeboards

Campus noticeboards have notices offering employment and accommodation. Find the student services area on campus and check out this information. Sometimes you'll have to be a local student before using this service but ask around and you may find some useful assistance or advice from staff.

Door knocking and gate calling

Door knocking or gate calling literally means seeking work by approaching the employer directly. With the correct dress, experience and confidence, you might walk out of a meeting with your job! When you think about it, rather than waiting for your perfect job, you go out of your way to create employment for yourself. Many employers perceive your efforts as showing initiative, confidence and determination; and may consider you as just the person they are looking for. At the very least, your name and contact details can be left in case a suitable position becomes available. So go to it but be prepared for the knock backs.

Employment agencies

Finding a good employment agency may mean the end to your search for work for the duration of your travels around Australia. Agencies seek both skilled and unskilled workers for just about any job imaginable. In fact, you will find many agencies spending their advertising dollar on advertisements in backpacker publications, which indicates their favourable attitude in seeking you out for employment.

Your first contact with an agency is extremely important. You must set the right impression from the beginning, which includes the way you dress, speak and, importantly, the way your resume is presented. The best tip when meeting staff from the agency is to aim to be remembered. You will be one of many people seeking employment through the agency, so it is always good to build a positive relationship with the agency staff. If you are short listed for a position, the agency staff will more times than not have some influence in the decision, so a sincere, personable and friendly approach will ensure you are presented in the best light possible.

Many agencies specialise in specific areas of employment, such as hospitality, office work, low-skilled work in factories and the building industry. Apart from the listings in this book, scan the yellow pages telephone directory in the city where you are seeking work. Also check out the employment section of the major newspapers mentioned above. The job advertisement may not be exactly what you are looking for, but other similar positions may be held exclusively by that agency. Many positions are not advertised because the agency may have enough people on their files to begin interviewing without the need for advertising. So, ensure you follow-up with the agencies that advertise in areas that appeal to you and get yourself known.

Below are 12 employment agencies, listed alphabetically, that have been included because they either offer walk-in offices in more than one state, or they are particularly interesting, unusual and more likely to appeal to working travellers.

Drake International

Level 7, 111 Gawler Place, Adelaide SA 5000. Tel: (08) 9321 9911. Email: adel@au.drakeintl.com. Website: www.drakeintl.com.

Drake International is a large personnel recruitment agency that covers practically every career. They have offices all over Australia and for detailed information, you should checkout their website at www.drakeintl.com. Areas covered include: office, professional contracting, industrial, medical and nursing services, information technology, call centre staff and engineering. With offices around Australia, they cater for overseas travellers wanting some flexibility in their working opportunities, both in the cities and rural areas.

DSC Placements

Unit 9/888 Bourke Street, Waterloo NSW 2017. Tel: (02) 9319 3766. Email: marketing@dscpersonnel.com.au. Website: www.dscpersonnel.com.au.

DSC Personnel is an Australian owned and operated business providing contract labour for over 20 years. The majority of placements are in the Sydney and Brisbane areas and overseas travellers are always welcome to apply for temporary positions.

Future Prospects

Level 15, Kindersley House, 33 Bligh Street, Sydney NSW 2000. Tel: (02) 9223 3033. Email: mail@future-prospects.net. Website: www.future-prospects.net.

Future Prospects mostly fills IT positions in Sydney CBD and North Sydney. They also have a division called Mac People which recruits desktop publishing and graphic design staff.

Hays Personnel

Level 1, 395 Collins Street, Melbourne VIC 3000. Tel: 1800 805 051. Website: www.hays.com.au.

Hays Recruitment Services is ranked in the world's top 10 largest recruitment consultancies. They are so big they have split up their services into: Hays Accountancy, Hays Metier (permanent and temporary office support), Hays Banking, Hays IT, Hays Montrose (property and construction industries), Hays Call Centre and Hays Executive. They operate in 22 locations throughout Australia and New Zealand and employ over 4500 temporaries everyday. Their website has plenty of useful information including salary information.

IPA Personnel

Level 20, IBM Centre 60 Centre Road, Southbank VIC 3006. Tel: (03) 9252 2222. Email: ipa@ipagroup.com.au. Website: www.ipagroup.com.au.

IPA Personnel is a nationwide personnel agency specialising in administration, accounts, clerical support, data entry, word processing, secretarial, call centre sales and customer service. They have been around for over 17 years and look to overseas backpackers to fill short-term and long-term positions. Some experience is necessary for most positions.

JANCO Educational Services

Suite 3, 46 Tennyson Road, Mortlake NSW 2137. Tel: (02) 9743 2155. Email: jan@janco.com.au. Website: www.janco.com.au.

Among other activities, JANCO maintains a database of qualified ESL teachers who are available on short notice to teach English as a second language to students in the Sydney region. They've got a comprehensive website listing all activities undertaken by the company, first established in 1999.

Jonathon Wren

Level 3, 5 Elizabeth Street, Sydney NSW 2000. Tel: (02) 9246 6422. Email: sydney@jwren.com.au. Website: www.jwren.com.au.

Jonathon Wren is part of the Addeco group of companies and they specialise in banking, finance and accounting placements around Australia. Their website is full of useful information and there is a section for UK candidates looking for work in Australia. Areas include a job search, immigration information, accommodation and travel advice—a very thorough overview for the traveller.

Other offices

Suite 3 Level 3, 69 Phillip Street, Parramatta NSW 2150. Tel: (02) 9865 6500.

Ground Floor, 350 Collins Street, Melbourne VIC 3000. Tel: (03) 9963 6300.

Level 13, 307 Queen Street, Brisbane QLD 4000. Tel: (07) 3287 8155.

Michael Page

Level 7, 1 Margaret Street, Sydney NSW 2000. Tel: (02) 8292 2000. Email: sydney@michaelpage.com.au. Website: www.michaelpage.com.au.

Michael Page International is a large recruitment firm with over 50 offices worldwide. Their comprehensive website is worth visiting.

Packers Palace

153 Hoddle Street, Richmond VIC 3121. Tel: (03) 9428 5932.

A small business that caters specifically to backpackers looking for work. Much of the work is unskilled including setting up equipment for event management companies, painting and rubbish removal. They also have some restaurant work available.

PGA Personnel

1st Floor, Pastoral House, 277 Great Eastern Highway Belmont WA 6104. Tel: (08) 9479 4599. Email: pga@pgaofwa.org.au. Website: www.pgaofwa.org.au.

PGA Personnel has been operating for over 70 years in the business of supplying companies with additional staff for both long-term and short-term project work. The job placements are Australia-wide and include positions for housekeepers, farm hands, cooks, tractor drivers, roadhouse staff and hotel staff. Before you leave home, you can download a registration form from their website and fax it back to them, along with a resume, to get the ball rolling before you arrive. Work visas are a must and placements are for between four and 12 weeks and normally include food and board. You will however, need to get to the job under your own steam.

Select Appointments

Select House, Level 14, 109 Pitt Street, Sydney NSW 2000. Tel: (02) 8258 9999. Email: selsyd@select-appointments.com.au. Website: www.select-appointments.com.au.

This is one big recruitment company that covers nearly every possible industry. They have split their company into: Select Appointments (providing a broad range of human resource services), Select Outplacement (supports companies that need to move employees out of the company), Select Payroll (outsourced payroll services), Select Teleresources (deals with telesales), Select Temporary and Select Travel (provides permanent, temporary and contract staff to the travel and tourism industry). Their website is full of valuable information and they have offices in Melbourne, Sydney, Newcastle, Brisbane and Perth.

Travel Personnel

Level 4, 115 Pitt Street, Sydney NSW 2000. Tel: (02) 9233 9955. Email: employment@travelpersonnel.com.au. Website: www.travelpersonnel.com.au.

If you are a travel agent or have airline experience, Travel Personnel can set you up with temporary work. Travel Personnel was founded in 1994 and is Sydney's number one source of temporary and permanent travel staff. The staff have a good knowledge of every sector of the travel industry, including corporate, leisure, airlines, wholesale, travel IT and inbound tourism. Whether you are looking for short-term temp position or contract work they can help.

Volunteer work

A number of voluntary options are discussed in this chapter. By participating in voluntary work, you have an opportunity to meet other people who have made a conscious decision to (in many cases) pay a nominal amount of money to participate in a structured program for the benefit of others or planet earth. For this reason, the motivation goes above and beyond the need to make money, and other priorities such as sharing in a worthwhile project with like-minded people may be your reason for signing up.

Australian Sports Camps

Australian Sports Camps offer coaching in cricket, tennis, football and netball at all levels for children aged six to 17 years. The coaching is undertaken by professional coaches and guest elite Australian and international players. Australian Sports Camps have been operating for over 18 years throughout Australia and have had over 35,000 boys and girls participating from all corners of Australia.

Camps operate during the July school holidays and Christmas holidays in December and January. Positions (both voluntary and paid) are on offer to enthusiastic applicants. Little skill is required in respect to sports, as the positions generally involve assisting in setting up equipment, providing beverages to the kids and other general duties.

Contact details

Australian Sports Camps, PO Box 1001, Upwey VIC 3158. Tel: (03) 9754 4455. Website: www.australiansportscamps.com.au.

Camp Australia

In 1987, Camp Australia's current directors, Anthony and Andrew Phillips, established an exclusive sports coaching service at Geelong Grammar School, Glamorgan, known as Phillips' Sports Coaching. Recognising the opportunity to conduct sport and recreation camps during the school holiday periods, the Phillips brothers created a series of innovative holiday entertainment camps for primary school students. The company, now operating as, Camp Australia, offers a smorgasbord of services for children aged between five and 18 years. Over 400 day and live-in camps have been held involving over 20,000 school aged children.

Camp Australia Camps

- Camp Australia FUN Camps (ages five to 12 years).
- Camp Australia Sports Camps (ages eight to 16 years).

Additional services:

- sports coaching
- special events
- child care

Camp Australia offers opportunities for qualified, energetic and enthusiastic individuals. Voluntary fieldwork experience, as well as paid positions, are offered in seasonal recruitment drives.

You can apply by completing the online application form or by forwarding a resume to the Camp Australia office. All suitable applicants will be contacted for an interview. Applicants with specific qualifications for particular sports or roles and with personalities displaying friendliness, enthusiasm, energy, patience and commitment will be highly regarded.

Contact details

Visit the Camp Australia website to find current employment opportunities at www.campaustralia.com.au.

Conservation Volunteers Australia (CVA)

CVA is Australia's largest practical conservation organisation. Each year CVA completes more than 1500 conservation projects across Australia. Volunteers perform all of CVA's conservation work and the organisation welcomes anyone who has a love of the outdoors and an interest in the environment. You can be young or old, Australian or a traveller from overseas and of any ability.

As an CVA volunteer you are part of a team of six to 10 willing participants. You work together to conserve a part of Australia's unique habitat. As well as making a real difference to helping the environment, it is a great way to make friends. The other volunteers on your team might be travellers, Australian university students, or locals who have lived in the area for years.

Each project is lead by an CVA team leader who provides all the training you need. Depending on where the project is located, accommodation might be in tents under the desert stars or in a cabin in the mountains. After a days work you get together with your fellow volunteers to chew the fat, experience Australian bush delights or surprise each other with samples of your home cooking!

A normal work day?

There is no such thing as an average day during your CVA conservation experience, but you can generally expect to be working on a project from 8 a.m. until 4 p.m. with breaks in the morning and afternoon, and for lunch, however times will depend on the climate.

When and where?

ACV projects run throughout the year across Australia and the best way to find out what is coming up is to visit the website below or call the free call number. The project length varies from one day to a week. All overnight projects cost $22 (or $11 concession) per night. This includes all food, accommodation and project related travel.

Contact details

There are 22 offices around Australia with the head office being in Ballarat, Victoria. Tel: Within Australia free call 1800 032 501 or (03) 5330 2600. Website: www.conservationvolunteers.com.au.

WWOOF

By Beth Allen

Australia is a wonderful country in which to travel. You can see Australia in a number of ways: by staying in the tried and true spots with other travellers, or you can experience the real Australia by living and working with families all over the country. WWOOF started in England in 1972 and was initially called Working Weekends on Organic Farms, but was changed to Willing Workers on Organic Farms when people started asking why only weekends?

Today there are WWOOF groups in 23 countries and WWOOF host farms scattered throughout these countries. All WWOOF groups are independent, but operate in a similar way when putting people in contact with the host farms. The WWOOF philosophy is the same worldwide: WWOOF hosts provide food and accommodation to people travelling in exchange for between four and six hours works per day.

WWOOF Australia began in 1982, and over the last 20 or so years has grown into an organisation that publishes a directory with over 1600 host farms and properties all over Australia. From suburban backyards in Cairns, to vast cattle stations in outback Australia, from Broome to Byron Bay. How about mustering cattle, cruising for crocodiles, building a straw bale bungalow, or feeding baby kangaroos? Fancy travelling up the East Coast of Australia on a yacht with one of our hosts? No mowing or weeding there!

Stay near some of the most beautiful national parks in the country like the Great Barrier Reef and the Grampians as well as other spectacular and remote out of the way places. WWOOF offers all this and more. With WWOOF you meet and stay with people who can virtually offer all this in their backyards—they know these areas and are willing to share them with you.

Purchasing a WWOOF book gives you membership of WWOOF and an insurance policy should you injure yourself whilst working on a registered WWOOF host property. This directory provides contact details of each property, the work to be done and details of the accommodation and food arrangements. The WWOOFer simply browses through the list, chooses a place they would like to visit, then contacts the host to arrange a mutually suitable time to visit. WWOOFers live and work with the host families in the same way as relatives and friends do when they visit.

The work is as varied as the farms. There are huge organic wheat farms, small co-operatively owned communities and people living alternative lifestyles growing their own food in order to live simply.

Many lifelong friendships are forged between the hosts and WWOOFers. WWOOFing changes and enriches people's lives. A young English WWOOFer came to Australia for a holiday without much gardening experience, spent some time on an organic farm, and became so enthused with all the new knowledge, that she returned home to study organic agriculture.

WWOOF is a not-for-profit organisation. Any surplus funds go back to the WWOOF hosts in the form of grants to enable them to carry out important conservation projects and reforestation works. WWOOFing is also a chance to learn about organic farming and environmental rehabilitation.

Contact details

WWOOF, 2166 Gelantipy Road, via W Tree, Buchan VIC 3885. Email: wwoof@wwoof.com.au. Tel: (03) 5155 0218 Website: www.wwoof.com.au.

Involvement Volunteers Assoc. Inc. (IVI)

IVI is a not-for-profit, non-government organisation that identifies suitable volunteer placements for individuals wishing to participate in volunteer activities in Australia or around the world.

Contact details

IVP, PO Box 218, Port Melbourne VIC 3207. Tel/Fax: (03) 9646 5504. Email: ivworldwide@volunteering.org.au. Website: www.volunteering.org.au.

International Volunteers for Peace (IVP)

IVP is the Australian arm of Civil Service International and as such is the place to sign up for workcamps overseas. However, there is an increasing number of workcamps in Australia for which IVP is always looking for volunteers. These workcamps are usually of short duration and consist of a number of participants involved in a particular project.

Contact details

International Volunteers for Peace, 499 Elizabeth Street, Surry Hills NSW 2010. Tel: (02) 9699 1129. Email: admin@ivp.org.au. Website: www.ivp.org.au.

Australian Volunteers International (AVI)

Better known for its placement of volunteers overseas, AVI also recruits volunteers to work in Australia, mostly in isolated Aboriginal settlements where a range of skills is needed, but not locally available.

Contact details

Australian Volunteers International, PO Box 350, Fitzroy VIC 3065. Tel: (03) 9279 1788. Email: info@australianvolunteers.com. Website: www.australianvolunteers.com.

National Seniors Association

In late 2006 the federal government announced the funding of the Senior Volunteer for Indigenous Communities program. The idea is that 'grey nomads' travelling the country with appropriate skills are able to sign up and be placed in an Aboriginal community for a period of time to assist set up or run something from a particular program to an ongoing operation. The idea is not only to pass on skills but also to allow relationships between the two groups to be established. This program will be run by the National Seniors Association. Check their website at www.nationalseniors.com.au for details.

Using the web

www.volunteeringaustralia.org

The website of Volunteering Australia, the national peak organisation for organisations and individuals active in the area. There is a link to www.govolunteer.com.au, a database of volunteer positions that are available in addition to links to state and regional volunteer centres.

www.volunteersearch.gov.au

This is a government website that allows those interested to search for volunteer positions around Australia.

www.volunteer.com.au

SEEK Volunteer is a non-profit initiative designed to bring volunteers and the organisations seeking them together. Volunteer opportunities are updated.

For working holiday makers

Overview

The working holiday program enhances the cultural and social development of young people, promotes mutual understanding between Australia and other nations and is an important part of the tourist industry.

Working holiday makers have a positive effect on the Australian economy. Based on 80,000 annual arrivals, it is estimated that working holiday makers spend around $1.3 billion annually.

The working holiday program also assists Australian employers by ensuring they have access to a large pool of seasonal workers and do not need to resort to recruiting illegal workers.

Working holiday visa

Australia's working holiday program allows working holiday makers to have an extended holiday in Australia by supplementing their travel funds through incidental employment while experiencing closer contact with local communities.

Australia has reciprocal working holiday arrangements with Belgium, Canada, Cyprus, Denmark, Estonia, Finland, France, Germany, Hong Kong, Ireland, Italy, Japan, Korea, Malta, Netherlands, Norway, Sweden, Taiwan and the UK.

Most applicants for a first working holiday visa are able to apply anywhere outside Australia. However, passport holders from the following countries can only lodge first working holiday visa applications in their home country: Japan, Korea, Malta, Cyprus, Taiwan and Hong Kong. Second working holiday visa applications may be made from any location either in or outside Australia.

The reciprocal nature of the working holiday agreements ensure young Australians are also offered similar opportunities by working overseas.

The second working holiday visa

Working holiday makers who have worked as a seasonal worker in an eligible regional Australian area for a minimum of three months while on their first working holiday visa will be eligible to apply for a second working holiday visa. Seasonal work for the purposes of the second working holiday visa is defined below:

Seasonal work is any type of work that is seasonal in nature or that is undertaken as the employee of a primary producer, including:

- plant and animal cultivation
- harvesting and/or packing of fruit and vegetable crops
- pruning and trimming vines and trees
- general maintenance crop work, cultivating or propagating plants, fungi or their products or parts
- immediate processing of plant products, maintaining animals for the purpose of selling them or their bodily produce, including natural increase
- immediate processing of animal products including shearing
- manufacturing dairy produce from raw material
- fishing and pearling
- conducting operations relating directly to taking or catching fish and other aquatic species
- conducting operations relating directly to taking or culturing pearls or pearl shell
- tree farming and felling
- planting or tending trees in a plantation or forest that are intended to be felled
- felling trees in a plantation or forest
- transporting trees or parts of trees that were felled in a plantation or forest to the place where they are first to be milled or processed

or from which they are to be transported to the place where they are to be milled or processed.

Over the last five years, the number of visas available under the working holiday-makers scheme have swelled from 35,000 in 1994-1995 to 113,936 in 2005-2006.

In 2005-06 most working holiday makers came from the following countries:

United Kingdom	28,821
Korea	24,077
Ireland	12,554
Germany	12,089
Japan	9,415
Canada	6,828
France	6,126

Working holiday visa criteria

Applicants for the first working holiday visa need to be:

- eligible passport holders
- aged between 18 and 30 (inclusive) at time of applying
- not have dependent children.

They should have a return ticket or sufficient funds for a return or onward fare as well as sufficient funds for the initial stage of their stay. All first working holiday visa applications must be made outside Australia. First working holiday visa holders are permitted a stay of 12 months from date of initial entry to Australia regardless of whether or not they spend the whole period in Australia.

Second working holiday visa applications

Second working holiday visa applications may be made from either in or outside Australia. To meet the requirements for the second working holiday visa, applicants will need to continue to meet the criteria for a working holiday visa outlined above, and have evidence of their three months of employment as a seasonal worker in regional Australia.

For second working holiday visa applications made outside Australia, working holiday makers are permitted a stay of 12 months from date of initial entry to Australia regardless of whether or not they spend the whole period in Australia. For second working holiday visa applications made inside Australia, the length of stay permitted depends on the type of visa held at the time of application. If the applicant holds a first working holiday visa when they apply, their second working holiday visa will permit them a total stay in Australia of 24 months from the date they first arrived on their first working holiday visa. If the applicant holds any other type of visa when they apply, their second working holiday visa will allow them a stay of 12 months from the date of grant. Any changes to these regulations can be found at www.immi.gov.au, the website of the Department of Immigration and Multicultural Affairs.

Earnings, income tax and superannuation

Working holiday makers should be paid the same rate of pay that is paid to locals, regardless of the formula. On the harvest trail you'll be paid by volume picked or by time, in hospitality jobs for example, you'll be paid by hours worked, usually on a part-time or casual rate. Rules regarding employment are the prerogative of the states so some of the rules and levels of pay will vary from state to state. Taxation is a federal government responsibility and there are some different rules regarding the payment of income tax by non-residents compared to locals and these are outlined below.

Before beginning work, you'll need to get a Tax File Number (TFN). To do this you'll need to visit a branch of the Australian Tax Office (ATO) taking your passport and another form of identification with you. You'll find the nearest branch by looking up the telephone book, asking around or checking ATO's website at www.ato.gov.au.

As a non-resident, your tax rate will be 29 per cent from the first dollar earned until you reach $25,000. You will therefore miss out on what is called the Tax Free Threshold, which allows Australian residents to earn their first $6000 tax free. Make sure your employer takes tax out from the first dollar you earn, otherwise you may end up owing the ATO money. Your tax rates are as follows:

$1 to $25,000		29%
$25,001 to $75,000	$7,250	+ 30%
$75,001 to $150,000	$22,250	+ 40%

You may be in a position to claim back income tax paid when you leave (the Australian financial year ends on 30 June) and the best way to do this is to make use of a tax agent, several of whom specialise in the requirements of short-term workers in Australia including working holiday makers. One such agency is the Laburnum Tax Agency in Melbourne (PO Box 5078, Laburnum Vic 3130. Tel: (03) 9894 2864. Email: labtax@bigpond.net.au.)

In attempt to bolster an increasingly inadequate government pension upon retirement, the federal government requires all employers to contribute nine per cent of an employee's pay (i.e. in addition to the pay) into each employee's superannuation fund. This rule applies once you are earning over $450 in gross wages per calendar month. There are new rules now offering overseas workers an opportunity to receive back their superannuation without having to wait until 55 or 60 years of age. For those intending to work for much of their time in Australia, it's worthwhile checking out this new ruling by getting in touch with your superannuation fund prior to leaving Australia to find out more about your options. (Your first employer may nominate a superannuation fund for you or give you a choice.) For the latest information regarding superannuation, go to ATO's website at www.ato.gov.au but generally speaking, if you hold a working holiday makers visa, you should be eligible to claim back your superannuation, less withholding tax by filling in forms found on the ATO's website or at any of their offices.

The bottom line with all this is that if you wish to keep a track of your earnings, your income tax payments and possible refunds, and your superannuation payments; you need to keep an accurate record of these as you go. Unless you have a photographic memory, you certainly won't remember it in six months time. Be consistent about recording details in a notebook and retaining the paperwork. If you're not fussed about it then don't worry especially if you don't intend to do much work.

Travel and medical insurance

The old saying 'if you can't afford travel insurance, you can't afford to travel' applies as much to Australia as it does to any other country, even if you are able to make use of the Australian public health system. You'll still need to cover yourself for theft, serious accident, emergency air tickets in the case of the death of a family member and other benefits of travel insurance. Citizens of the UK, New Zealand, Sweden, Netherlands, Malta, Italy and Finland can make use of some basic public health services while in Australia. Maltese and Italians can only make use of this arrangement for the first six months of their visit while all others can make use of the arrangement for the period of their stay in Australia.

So if you fit the above criteria, your next step is to sign up for Medicare (www.medicareaustralia.gov.au) when you arrive in Australia, by simply visiting your nearest Medicare customer service centre with your passport and evidence (i.e. healthcare card) that you are enrolled in your own country's national health scheme. Just to be sure, before leaving home, call your national health scheme to make sure you take the appropriate documents for enrolment in Australia. For a local call anywhere in Australia you can contact the Medicare Information Service on 13 20 11 for any questions.

Money

Travelling around Australia with a combination of cash, travellers cheques and a credit card will make it very easy to obtain your money when required. If you intend to stay for the full 12 months and to work then having a bank account with a local bank will be essential. Some of your employers will want to pay you by direct credit to your bank account while others will give you a cheque. The four major banks in Australia are the Commonwealth Bank, National Australia, Westpac and the ANZ. The Commonwealth Bank used to be government owned and so it has the best coverage across Australia of the four banks and you can make deposits and withdrawals from most post offices as well. Although there are a number of smaller banks you should open an account with one of these banks.

The main credit cards used in Australia are Visa, MasterCard, American Express and Diners Club though the last two have only a small market share. It's best to carry either a Visa or MasterCard (or a partner card such as Eurocard). Don't try and travel around Australia only with an American Express or Diners Club card. You'll be able to use your credit card for purchases just about everywhere. If you belong to a frequent purchase scheme you may wish to make most of your purchases on your credit card. The price for cash and credit used to be the same, but recently rules have changed and purchases on credit cards may cost slightly more, especially in country areas. You'll be able to use your card in automatic teller machines (ATMs) which are very common, but note, that if you use an ATM that is not one of your bank's ATMs, you'll be charged a fee of about $1 to $1.50. This is another reason to open an account with the Commonwealth Bank because it has more ATMs than other banks. EFTPOS facilities are also common but you'll need to keep your savings account (if that is your EFTPOS account) topped up to avoid rejections. Both the use of credit cards and EFTPOS facilities are convenient but these will often end up costing more than paying in cash. You'll need to make a choice. In case of theft make sure you always have an alternative arrangement for getting hold of your money.

Electrical appliances

Australia has an electrical current of 240 volts with 50 Hz. European electrical appliances used to feeding off 220 volts will be happy, but North American appliances will feel a bit burnt out and will require a transformer. The local plug is a lightweight one with three flat pins and overseas appliances will need an adaptor. If you have-not purchased an adaptor before arriving you'll should find one in large department stores, some outdoor shops or travel agents.

Driving

The first thing working holiday makers will notice about the roads is that Australians drive on the left-hand side. If you come from a country that drives on the right-hand side and intend to purchase or rent a vehicle, you'll have to discipline your automatic responses. (And then do the same when you get home.) The cost of petrol will be cheap for Europeans but a bit expensive for those from Canada and the US. It will quickly become more expensive the further you get from a capital city and more so as you travel inland. Sharing the cost with others is a good way to go.

You should arrive with an international drivers permit as well as your drivers licence both to drive in Australia and to use as a second form of identification if required. If you do decide to purchase a car (along with appropriate insurance) you should also join the state motorist's association as soon as you purchase a vehicle. Membership is of great use if you breakdown and have no local assistance (and no tools). The following is a list of the state organisations and their websites. Membership of one state association automatically provides assistance in other states.

Queensland: RACQ – www.racq.com.au.

New South Wales: NRMA – www.nrma.com.au.

Victoria: RACV – www.racv.com.au.

Tasmania: RACT Tasmania – www.ract.com.au.

South Australia: RAA – www.raa.net.

Western Australia: RACWA – www.rac.com.au.

Northern Territory: AANT has no website but information can be gained by ringing the Darwin office on (08) 8981 3837.

Keeping in touch

You'll find internet cafes just about everywhere including many hostels. Some hostels now offer additional services like photocopying, mail services and employment boards. You'll find lists of internet cafes in the *TNT Magazine* and other free publications distributed throughout the backpacker network. You should definitely speak to other travellers for the latest place to hang out and download your email from home. You shouldn't need to pay too much for access and in fact many backpacker travel agents now offer free limited access as a way to attract your business.

If you intend to pack your laptop then you can sign up for various wireless deals around Australia. In the outback the only form of internet communication via your laptop—a satellite phone—will be very expensive. MacDonalds have wireless hotspots in many of their more popular outlets. Check out http://whirlpool.net.au for information on deals and technical issues.

Australia Post is much more than just a place to post letters. It is even possible to order goods over the internet and arrange to pick these up at a post office which is a great idea for the backpacker who may be in transit or simply of no fixed address. Apart from this service and the many things you can buy in Australia Post mini-shops, the traditional Post Restante concept still applies in Australia. You can have family and friends mail you a package or letter directly to a nominated post office addressed to you c/o Poste Restante. Mail will be held for four weeks. Simply roll up with your passport for identification and pick up your mail.

Apart from post offices, many backpacker businesses offer mail holding and forwarding. One such business is Landbase Australia that offers travellers a personalised mail holding and forwarding service to anywhere in the world. The service costs approximately $30 per month and you pay a credit amount in advance to cover the cost of postage for any initial mail forwarding, then just top up your account when it gets low. The service is operated by Jan, who has considerable experience travelling by yacht and therefore understands the need for a reliable mail service for travellers. Landbase. Tel: 0408 686 461 (between 9:00 and 17:00 Eastern Standard Time). Email: 1base@ozemail.com.au. Website: www.ozemail.com.au/~lbase.

Other organisations, including most backpacker specialist travel agents, offer a similar service including:

International Exchange Programs, Level 3, 333 George Street, Sydney NSW 2000. Tel: (02) 9299 0400.

Travellers Contact Point, Level 7, Dymocks Building, 428 George Street, Sydney NSW 2000. Tel: (02) 9221 8744.

Tourist Refund Scheme (TRS)

Since July 2000 tourists departing Australia can claim a refund for taxes paid on a particular item worth more than $300 or on goods individually worth less than that, but where the total purchase of these goods was made at one store and where the cost is more than $300. So if you purchased $250 worth of goods from one store, you are not eligible for a tax refund. In other words this scheme encourages you to make your purchases at one store in minimum lots of $300 in order to maximise your tax refund. In addition, the goods must be purchased no earlier than 30 days before leaving Australia. Make sure you retain documentary evidence of your purchases in the form of a tax invoice.

The taxes you are claiming back are the Goods and Services Tax (GST) and (maybe) the Wine Equalisation Tax (WET). However, this refund only applies to goods which travellers carry as hand luggage when leaving the country. It does not apply to services or goods consumed or partly consumed in Australia. The GST refund is calculated by dividing the total amount of the purchase by 11 (i.e. 10 per cent of the cost of the goods). The WET refund is 14.5 per cent of the price paid for wine.

When leaving Australia, you will find a TRS booth inside the passport control area of international terminals at Sydney, Brisbane, Melbourne, Perth, Cairns, Adelaide, Darwin and Coolangatta.

At the booth, you will need to produce the goods, the tax invoice from the retailer and your passport and boarding pass. The process will only take a few minutes however, you should allow for other passengers queuing for a refund so it is worthwhile checking in at least 15 minutes earlier. Refunds will be available until 30 minutes before the aircraft is due to depart. Some goods are excluded from the scheme including alcohol other than wine, tobacco products, GST free goods, goods already wholly or partially consumed and goods not allowed on aircraft.

Organising work before you leave home

If you're reading this book at home and have yet to organise your trip to Australia there are some organisations that can help make it easy and in some cases, can assist setting up work before you arrive. There are some good reasons why you should consider this option. It may be your first time overseas and Mum and Dad would feel more confident if you are arranging your travel with an organisation that prepares many of your pre-departure tasks for you. They (and you!) may also feel more comfortable knowing, for instance, that on arrival in a foreign country you will have access to a 24-hour emergency telephone number. Or maybe that you will be travelling with other young people from your home country appeals, as you will arrive with a bunch of new friends to travel with.

For the seasoned traveller, maybe the packages offered by these travel organisations work out to be cheaper than if you went about buying your own air ticket, insurance and arrival accommodation. Not to mention that you will also have access to exclusive job listings on arrival and free beer on the first night at the new arrivals party! Whatever the reason, the following organisations offer some great value, as well as acting as a bit of a security blanket while you have the time of your life in Australia. However, at the end of the day you need to shop around to see what suits you best.

One large organisation with offices in many of the working holiday-maker countries is the Work and Travel Company. This outfit offers different packages combining elements of travel with paid work, volunteer work, study and internship programs in Australia.

Work and Travel Australia

This program has been designed for 18-30 year olds holding a working holiday maker visa and includes a couple of options for the participant from a complete package including airfares, insurance and arrival services, or for those already with an air ticket in hand, participants can take a slimmed down version which covers excellent support and services operated out of their Sydney office.

Volunteer and Travel Australia

For those looking for a rural experience this program offers participants the opportunity to work on conservation projects for a period ranging from two to six weeks at various locations around Australia.

Work and Study Australia – English language

Study programs range from two to 32 weeks with the possibility of obtaining the Cambridge Certificate or the London Chamber of Commerce Certificate in English Language Competency. Participants obtain a study visa for Australia which also allows them to work up to 20 hours per week for the duration of the course. Participants have access to the extensive employment services offered by the Work and Travel Company office in Sydney.

Internship Australia program

Through relationships with Australian-based organisations, the Work and Travel Company is able to offer intern positions for students, graduates and young professionals in chosen their career.

Work and Travel Company

Contact your nearest Work and Travel Company below for more information:

Netherlands

Work and Travel Company Holland, Travel Active, Postbus 107, 5800 AC Venray, The Netherlands. Tel: 0478 551 900. Email: info@travelactive.nl. Website: www. travelactive.nl.

Germany

Work and Travel Company Germany, STEP IN GmbH, Beethovenallee 21, 53173 Bonn, Germany. Tel: 0228 956 950. Email: info@step-in.de. Website: www.step-in.de.

Sweden

Work and Travel Company Sweden, Reseagenterna AB, Box 1090, Sundstorget 3, 3rd Floor, SE-251 10, Helsingborg, Sweden.

Tel: 042-17 95 25. Email: info@worktravel.org. Website: www.worktravel.org.

Denmark

Work and Travel Company Denmark, Rojumvej 66, DK-6400 Sonderborg, Denmark. Tel: 7442 1188. Email: info@alott.dk. Website: www.worktravelcompany.dk.

Norway

Work and Travel Company Norway, Markveien 1, N-0554 Oslo, Norway. Tel: 2235 8020. Email: info@ workandtravel.no. Website: www.worktravelcompany.no.

Finland

Work and Travel Company Finland, Aktiv-Resor Finland, Lonnrotinkatu 35, 00180 Helsinki, Finland. Tel: 09-612 40 658. Email: info@worktravelcompany.fi. Website: www.worktravelcompany.fi.

Iceland

Work and Travel Company Iceland, Stúdentaferðir/VistaXChange, Bankastraeti 10, 101 Reykjavik, Iceland. Tel: 01-562 2362. Website: www.vistaexchange.is.

Hong Kong

Work & Travel Company Hong Kong, Hong Kong Overseas Studies Centre, Room 829-830, Star House, 3 Salisbury Road, Tsim Sha Tsui, Kowloon, Hong Kong. Tel: 2730 2068. Email: info@worktravelcompany.com.hk. Website: www.worktravelcompany.com.hk.

UK

Work & Travel Company UK, International Employment & Training Ltd, 45 High Street, Tunbridge Wells, Kent TN1 1XL, England. Tel: 01892-516 164. Email: info@woktravelcompany.co.uk. Website: www.worktravelcompany.co.uk.

US

InterExchange, Inc., 161 Sixth Avenue, New York, NY 10013, USA. Tel: 0212-924 0446. Email: work abroad@interexchange.org. Website: www.interexchange.org/workingabroad.

Other Organisations

Canada

SWAP Australia is a program run by the Canadian Federation of Students (CFS) in conjunction with Travel Cuts. You have the choice of travelling on a group flight or going by yourself. The SWAP Australia package includes pre-departure information, an orientation in Sydney and two nights accommodation upon arrival, a prearranged bank account, mail forwarding, phone card, an email service along with the working holiday visa and ongoing assistance. For more information contact SWAP or a Travel Cuts office near you. Check out SWAP's website at www.swap.ca.

Ireland

USIT Travel offers the Sydney and Melbourne starter packages for those travelling to Australia with a working holiday visa and booking through USIT in Ireland. For AU$65.00 the package includes an airport transfer, an orientation and two nights accommodation upon arrival in Australia. For more information contact a USIT office in Ireland, phone them on 01-602 1700 or visit their website at www.usit.ie.

Japan

Council Exchanges Japan runs an Australia work and travel program along the same lines as the one from run by Council Exchanges UK. For more information contact Council Exchanges Japan, 5-52-67 Jinguamae, Shibuya-ku, Tokyo 150-8355, Japan. Tel: 03-5467 5501. Email: info@cieej.or.jp. Website: www.cieej.or.jp.

More information

Travel guides

All major travel guides have a guide for Australia but Lonely Planet is on home ground in Australia and it's their biggest selling guide. The Rough Guides guide to Australia is also packed with information and caters to a similar audience as the Lonely Planet guide. Not to mention all the other guides. In the end it's your choice. Lonely Planet has guides for individual states and some regions, along with special interest guides like wildlife watching, cycling and bushwalking.

Maps

There are plenty of maps both of Australia as a whole, of states and of smaller areas. You'll find plenty of these maps in travel guides as well as at local tourist authorities. If you're in a car, a recommended map which is rather large but very easy to read is *The Penguin Touring Atlas of Australia*.

Giveaway publications

Apart from the free publications produced by tourist authorities the following magazines are both free and can be found throughout the packpacker network around Australia.

TNT Magazine produce three full-size monthly magazines, 'Sydney/NSW/ACT', 'Qld/Bryon Bay/NT' and 'Explorer' which covers the other four states. They also produce an email newsletter every two weeks. You can subscribe to this newsletter by going to their website at www.tntmag.com.au.

Travel Maps Australia produces the monthly *The Word: Backpacking Australia*. Check their website at www.tma.com.au.

Australiana

Apart from what you read in the destination travel guides the following is a snippet of suggested reading about Australia and it's people.

Aboriginal Australia & the Torres Strait Islands: a guide to Indigenous Australia, Lonely Planet, 2001. This book is the ideal introduction to the indigenous peoples of Australia and the Torres Strait islands.

Traveller's History of Australia, John Chambers. An easy to read overview of the birth and development of European Australia.

The Fatal Shore, Robert Hughes. An eye opener covering the brutality of transportation and the convict era of Australia.

Sydney, Jan Morris. An investigation and informative read on Australia's 'international city'.

Cloudstreet, Tim Winton. One of the most read recent novels from a favourite Australian author.

Other favourite Australian novels can be found by going to the Book Show's website on ABC Radio National at http://www.abc.net.au/radio/book.

Websites

www.yha.org.au YHA Australia, budget accommodation specialists.

www.nomadsworld.com Nomads is a budget accommodation provider with some hostels offering employment referrals in the local area.

www.ozex.com.au Oz Experience is a hop-on, hop-off backpackers bus service around Australia.

www.waywardbus.com.au Wayward Bus operates a hop-on hop-off bus service.

www.travellers-autobarn.com.au Travellers' Autobarn, located in NSW and Queensland, caters to the backpacker market.

www.wakeup.com.au The largest privately owned backpacker hostel in the world with 500 beds. Large but with a personnel touch and right in the centre of Sydney.

www.footprintswestend.com.au Funky Accommodation located in heart of Sydney and only 5 minutes walk from Sydney Central Train & Bus Station offering beds from $21. Footprints Westend Sydney, 412 Pitt Street, Central Sydney. Freecall: 1800 013 186 or (02) 9211 4588.

www.worktravelcompany.com The Work and Travel Company International (WTCI) offers international work, language and volunteer programs in Australia, New Zealand and Latin America. They are represented by international partners working from countries that have or will have a working holiday agreement with Australia or New Zealand.

Appendix

School holidays

School holidays vary between states and territories. The school holidays always mean extra jobs in the more popular holiday regions to cope with the influx of visitors. Though many of these, especially in retail, may go to local school children, there are often vacancies. With the exception of winter where jobs in the snow are available, the general rule on the east coast of Australia and Tasmania is that holiday-makers move towards water and go north, though many go to the outback in winter when temperatures are cooler. In South Australia and Western Australia they go south towards water.

These dates apply to 2007 but will vary slightly from year to year.

	School starts	Easter break	Winter break	Spring break	School finishes
QLD	28 Jan	6 - 16 Apr	23 Jun - 9 Jul	22 Sep - 7 Oct	15 Dec
NSW	28 Jan	6 - 22 Apr	30 Jun - 15 Jul	29 Sep - 14 Oct	22 Dec
ACT	1 Feb	14 - 29 Apr	7-22 Jul	29 Sep - 14 Oct	22 Dec
VIC	29 Jan	31 Mar - 15 Apr	30 Jun - 15 Jul	22 Sep - 7 Oct	22 Dec
TAS	13 Feb	6 - 15 Apr	2 - 17 Jun	8 Sep - 23 Sep	varies between schools
SA	29 Jan	14 - 30 Apr	8 - 23 Jul	30 Sep - 15 Oct	16 Dec
WA	31 Jan	5 - 22 Apr	7 - 23 Jul	29 Sep - 15 Oct	14 Dec
NT	29 Jan	6 - 15 Apr	23 Jun - 23 Jul	29 Sep - 7 Oct	15 Dec

Population of cities and towns

Urban areas can be good hunting grounds for jobs especially with the low levels of unemployment currently experienced in Australia. The best work opportunities are in those areas expanding most rapidly which means northernWestern Australia and central Queensland. The following chart (not all are single cities or towns, some are a number of towns close together) gives you an idea of the amount of work that might be available based on population.

Rank	Statistical Division/District	Est. Population 2006
1	Sydney (NSW)	4,293,105
2	Melbourne (Vic)	3,684,461
3	Brisbane(Qld)	1,820,375
4	Perth (WA)	1,507,949
5	Adelaide (SA)	1,138,833
6	Gold Coast-Tweed Heads (Qld/NSW)	554,628
7	Newcastle (NSW)	512,131
8	Canberra (328,441)-Queanbeyan (ACT/NSW)	374,766
9	Wollongong (NSW)	276,155
10	Sunshine Coast (Qld)	220,199
11	Hobart (Tas)	205,510
12	Geelong (Vic)	167,781
13	Townsville (Qld)	153,631
14	Cairns (Qld)	127,856
15	Toowoomba (Qld)	121,612
16	Darwin (NT)	113,955
17	Launceston (Tas)	103,835
18	Albury-Wodonga (NSW/Vic)	101,273
19	Ballarat (Vic)	90,303
20	Bendigo (Vic)	85,978
21	Burnie-Devonport (Tas)	79,954
22	Mandurah (WA)	77,619
23	Latrobe Valley (Vic)	75,553
24	Mackay (Qld)	73,091

continues

Rank	Statistical Division/District	Est. Population 2006
25	Rockhampton (Qld)	70,128
26	Bundaberg (Qld)	62,457
27	Bunbury (WA)	59,033
28	Wagga Wagga (NSW)	54,191
29	Coffs Harbour (NSW)	50,368
30	Hervey Bay (Qld)	50,293
31	Mildura (Vic)	48,836
32	Shepparton (Vic)	48,063
33	Tamworth (NSW)	43,774
34	Gladstone (Qld)	43,507
35	Port Macquarie (NSW)	41,332
36	Orange (NSW)	37,982
37	Dubbo (NSW)	35,972
38	Nowra-Bomaderry (NSW)	33,364
39	Bathurst (NSW)	32,398
40	Lismore (NSW)	31,626
	Total = about 84% of Australia's population	16,703,877